A Short Introduction to
Language and
Language Teaching

A Short Introduction to
Language and
Language Teaching

with a comprehensive
glossary of terms

C. J. Brumfit and J. T. Roberts

Batsford Academic and Educational Ltd
London

© C. J. Brumfit and J. T. Roberts 1983
First published 1983

Typeset by Deltatype, Ellesmere Port
and printed in Great Britain by
Billing & Sons Ltd.,
Worcester ·
for the publishers
Batsford Academic and Educational Ltd
4 Fitzhardinge Street
London W1H 0AH

British Library Cataloguing in Publication Data
Brumfit, C. J.
    A short introduction to language and language
    teaching.
    1. Language acquisition   2. Language and
    education
    I. Title   II. Roberts, J. T.
    401'.9   P118

ISBN 0 7134 1599 1

Contents

1 Introduction: What do we need to know?

There are three possible approaches to the discussion of language teaching. One is to concentrate on the classroom exclusively, and to deal with techniques directly, with very little attempt to justify why one technique is chosen rather than another. This approach has its value, particularly when teachers are being prepared in a hurry for highly predictable situations, and it is often successful when able teachers pass on their accumulated professional wisdom to newcomers to the profession, who are more or less in the position of apprentices. It has the disadvantage that teachers sometimes find it difficult to adapt to new and different situations: no techniques can be transferred independently of the characters of the teachers and the pupils, and teachers need to be fairly self-conscious about what they are doing (at least for some of the time) in order to make a successful selection from their repertoire of techniques. To do this requires them to have some explicitly formulated principles on which their teaching is based.

A second approach, then, would concentrate on the principles rather than on the classroom itself. This also has its dangers, because it is very easy to interpret principles as statements which can be lectured on, or read up from books. Teaching courses based on principles may appear to be more academically 'respectable' than practical courses; at the same time, they may in fact be far away from the classroom, so that the principles become divorced from any serious activity concerned with pupils.

A third approach is to try to integrate the two approaches mentioned above: to expect teachers to master all the fundamental practical skills, but at the same time to expect them to be able to see the strengths and weaknesses of all the techniques at their disposal, so that they can justify exactly what they are doing at any one moment in their lesson. This means that they will constantly be aware of such matters as: What are the aims of this lesson? What justification is there for choosing such an aim? What techniques will be successful, on the basis of past experience, in achieving this aim? What implications will the choice of one technique have for later work in the same lesson? And so on. Generalising slightly, the first approach concentrates on doing, the second on knowing, and the third on the relationship between knowing and doing. This book is based on the third approach, but it cannot enable the reader to 'do' in itself. What it can provide is an introductory source of the basic knowledge which must always interact with classroom decisions and actions. The purpose of this chapter is to introduce the various areas of linguistic knowledge which are essential for the language teacher.

Knowing how to do things

Since teachers' prime aim is to teach, their main concern will be with actions. These actions may take place either inside or outside the classroom, but they will be things which are done, directly or indirectly, to make the process of learning languages as effective as possible for all pupils. A great part of the process of training to be a teacher, therefore, must consist of acquiring practical skills. However, these will not be the skills which are used in the classroom alone, and nor will they be only the skills which are superficially apparent to a casual observer.

Supposing we consider an apparently very simple classroom event, for example the moment when a teacher starts to ask pupils some questions about a new piece of work which he has just introduced. If we think about this for a moment, it will at once become apparent that the teacher has had to make three types of decision: *what* to do, *when* to do it, and *how* to do it. Nor do these questions necessarily have to be answered in this order. For example, a teacher may realise that the class is becoming bored with a particular piece of work, and decide to change the pattern of activity before he has decided exactly what change he is going to make. Alternatively, he may decide that the technique he is using is not as effective as he would like, and may want to try something more effective. In these cases, he must draw upon a wide range of techniques which he will have at his fingertips, select from that range the most appropriate for his needs, and adapt it to the particular situation of his class, the time of day, the aids and facilities available, his own feelings and energy at that moment, and any other relevant factors. The teacher in the example given above needs to know how to formulate the questions most conveniently, how to ask them so that they achieve the desired result, how to choose the most suitable pupils for his immediate aim in the lesson, and whether to use his questions as a lead-in to further questions, or to some other type of questioning activity—for example pupil-pupil questioning, or simultaneous pairs work in which all the pupils are talking at once.

This may appear to be making a fairly simple activity into something unnecessarily complicated, and in one sense it is. People with a natural flair for teaching will soon—after a fairly short period of teaching—develop an ability to organise the class in the way they want. However, not everyone has this natural flair, and sometimes those who have are liable to confuse ability to organise the class well with ability to organise it for effective learning. It is usually helpful to ask *exactly* what is happening in a lesson. This involves understanding the mind of the pupil, as well as the mind of the teacher, the ways in which classrooms usually function, the nature of the subject matter of the lesson (in this case language) and many other features of the situation. Although we cannot understand everything about a class situation such as this (there are many things we simply do not know), we can nevertheless understand a certain amount. If we want our teaching to be thoroughly effective, we must make sure that our techniques and the way in which we use them are compatible with what we understand of how teaching and learning of languages takes place. Thus our learning how to *do* things is closely bound up with our knowledge about these things, with what we *know*.

Now, much of teachers' understanding derives from the combination of their experience with their knowledge of a large number of fields which are discussed in general education courses, for example the psychological needs of different sorts of pupils, the social implications of particular ways of organising classrooms, and so on. The language teacher has a special responsibility in relation to these, however, for language teachers are concerned with the medium of communication itself. Other teachers use language for teaching something else. Language teachers use it for teaching itself. The risk of this is that it may become quite unreal, because it is not used to say anything of the slightest interest to students, or—the other extreme

—that teachers will concentrate so heavily on content that they forget their role as teachers of the means of communication. Anyway, since language is our most subtle and complex means of self-expression, learning a new language or dialect, or extending our competence in our present language, is closely bound up with our own personal development. A language teacher must believe in extending the linguistic powers of pupils, but the teacher must also recognise that such extension must be made without forcing pupils to reject their present languages or dialects. The process of language development and change, at a personal level, needs to be seen as entirely natural—a product of our need to talk with people we want to talk to, and to read and write about things we want to read and write about. There is no virtue in knowing a lot about another language, or even in being able to use it, unless we can put our ability to use for purposes which we have chosen ourselves. So we need to help our students to do more than merely possess the language; we need to help them to use it enthusiastically, for their own needs.

As with any other sort of learning, teaching is best learnt through practice. No book can be a substitute for the combination of practice with a real class and the close support of an experienced teacher. However, a book can offer help in relating the knowledge which a teacher needs to practical problems, and it can also, of course, provide access to many of the arguments and ideas basic to a sensitive understanding of teaching. In this book, the main emphasis will be on the nature of human language, but of course the language teacher also needs to understand many other aspects of teaching which are common to all teaching situations.

Approaches to language study
There are many different ways of knowing about something. We very often feel we understand something because we have been familiar with it for a long time—as when we say we know a town well. That does not mean we can give long lists of statistics about its population, area and so on, but it does mean that in some sense we have a 'feel' for the place, and can distinguish it from other places which have a different 'feel'. One of the problems with the study of language is that—as we all speak at least one language—we have a very strong 'feel' for language which can sometimes interfere with our ability to perceive it objectively. Perceiving it objectively is not the only valid way of perceiving language—it is difficult to love

linguistic interference

'objectively' but some people clearly love language, as poets or even just as readers—but there is value and interest in trying to look at language objectively, just as there is interest in knowledge of the population-growth of large cities. For teachers it is particularly important to be able to know which facts about language are universal and which apply only to particular languages, for such information will have a direct bearing on their attitude to different learners. There is a more important reason why language teachers should be objectively interested in language, however, and that is that they are forced more and more to rely on decisions which are made on their behalf by administrators, text-book writers, syllabus-designers and others, and these decisions are usually based themselves on information about language which claims to be 'scientific' and 'objective'. If teachers want either to co-operate fully with those who influence language teaching—or to challenge them—they must be able to interpret the reasons for the decisions which are being made on their behalf. They are not merely making linguistic decisions themselves all the time, but they are also at the mercy of others who make the decisions for them. Their main protection is that they are fully informed themselves.

It is important to note, also, that we have been discussing the study of *language*, not of any particular language. All human beings, except for those who are prevented by some form of physical barrier, learn language naturally. It is therefore a biological phenomenon of great interest, as it is a characteristic of our species. If we are concerned with teaching foreign languages, we need to note also that, while some people learn foreign languages naturally, many others do not. Most of those who do not are to be found in schools and other language teaching institutions, precisely because these places claim to be able to make up for the lack of a natural situation in which to learn. The foreign language teacher is undertaking to teach something which many people do not need to be taught and to provide circumstances which will enable pupils to do something which they appear to be very well equipped to do, at an early stage in their life, with little overt teaching. Yet many people do fail to learn second languages. If we are going to make teaching as efficient as possible, we need to understand as much as possible about language, and especially about how successful learners learn it, and how it is that some people find learning it so difficult when it is not their mother tongue.

The last 80 years or so have seen a great deal of interesting and relevant work in linguistics, and it is the purpose of the first two sections of this book to introduce the main traditional concerns of linguistics and their relationship to language teaching. This means that we need to consider briefly why linguistics claims to be 'the scientific study of language'.

The scientific study of language

Science is concerned with establishing our knowledge as clearly as possible. The procedures which have been developed for the study of language have the purpose simply of enabling people to talk about language to each other as precisely as possible. This means that terminology used has to be clearly defined, and must not be confused with the less precise terminology of ordinary life—hence there is a language for talking *about* language. It means also that 'facts' that are established about language need to be expressed in such a way that other linguists can understand them without confusion and can follow the argument, or the experiments which led to the establishment of the 'facts', in such a way that they can repeat the processes and test whether they are valid, and whether the conclusions are justified by the evidence. It means that the processes for the investigation of language have to be made explicit and that a great deal of time should be spent in thinking as clearly as possible about the questions which can and cannot be investigated by linguistics. A scientific study of language will not enable us to say that one poem is definitely better than another one, so there is no point in asking that question—but it may give us the tools for discovering whether one poet's style is similar to another's in particular respects. What use that information is put to may be the province of the literary critic, but the objective information may be gathered with the linguist's tools. Other questions may be theoretically answerable, but may not be possible to answer for purely practical reasons, like the number of people who are literate in a given language. It is important to recognise which questions are inappropriate for linguistics, and which are appropriate but practically unanswerable, so that we can see the limits of its usefulness. In the effort to establish clearly what it is possible to know about language, a number of principles have been established which help us to think about this extremely complex phenomenon more straighforwardly.

Preface

The purpose of this book is to provide a succinct, straightforward and up to date introduction to language teaching. The first part attempts to provide answers to basic questions about the organisation of language: What is syntax? What is phonology? What is semantics? In the second part the social and psychological roles of language are outlined, and in the third part, the longest, important issues in mother tongue, foreign and second language teaching are discussed together with other general issues such as course design and testing. Extensive help in follow-up reading is also provided.

This is not a book to turn the reader into a good teacher—that can only come from experience in the classroom and from contact with other experienced teachers. But it does aim to introduce the reader to all the relevant knowledge necessary to convert interest and human sympathy into expertise. Of course such a short book can only be a beginning, but we hope that it will prove useful to those who are starting to think about language teaching, and provide a series of convenient reference points for those who are continuing to develop, by experience or study. One or two chapters, for example those on stylistics or technology, may not be of immediate interest to some beginners, but it seemed worthwhile to include some brief discussion of the most important issues for those who develop interests in these directions. Altogether, the book is based on the belief that teachers who do not know as much as possible about the nature of language, of people as they use language, and of various different approaches to the teaching of language, will lessen their chances of self-improvement and increase the risk of falling prey to fashion and the whims of the market.

We have drawn on our own experience of teaching, on reading, and on discussions with colleagues and students, in an attempt to report, as simply as possible, the current state of our understanding of language and language teaching. We have tried to avoid matters which are still controversial to linguists and other scientists, and concentrated on what is commonly accepted by the most informed members of the teaching profession. At the same time, we believe that most of what we have to say is important for all types of language teaching, and—furthermore—that language teachers of all types have much to learn from each other. Consequently we have included discussion of mother tongue, second language and foreign language teaching, and we hope that readers will compare the concerns of colleagues with their own.

One final note of clarification: this book does not provide discussion of teaching techniques, and readers who wish to acquire ideas for classroom activities should consult books referred to in our final chapter. It does aim to discuss all the major theoretical issues that should worry language teachers.

We would like to thank a number of readers who have made suggestions on the text, and our own colleagues and students, for their help.

CJB
JR

First, we recognise that we cannot grasp the rapid movement of language as it passes by. By some means, we have to stabilise it. At the beginning of this century the Swiss linguist, Saussure, pointed out that there are two ways of looking at a linguistic system. We could consider the history of its development, taking what is called a *diachronic* approach, or we could consider the system at a given moment, as it is now, for example, across the whole of the speaking community. This would be taking a *synchronic* approach.

Now the problem with a synchronic approach is that it is based on a fiction. In order to talk about the system of English at this moment we have to ignore a large number of questions which affect us in the real world. We have to ignore, for example, the fact that everyone speaks English slightly differently, the fact that many of the things that people say do not reflect exactly their knowledge of the grammar of the language (for example we leave sentences unfinished because we are in a hurry, or forgetful, or because we can see that our message has already been understood), and the fact that language varies according to the situation in which it is spoken. In order to generalise, we have to create a consistent and stable language which does not really exist for any single speaker. We create a *model* of the language which we are able to describe as a basis for discussion. Above this, we create a model of language in general, and we create models of how people learn languages, and of how they use them. Each of these is a generalisation, as clear as is possible for our purposes, based on our understanding of how the process works in many specific cases, or on our logical examination of how the process should work. More thought and more observational evidence will lead the models to change, but it is the general principles which such models illustrate which we need to apply to our specific language teaching situations if we want to evaluate our work as teachers.

Traditionally, what some people call *core linguistics,* because it represents the central core of the discipline, has concentrated on either descriptions of particular languages or the nature of the phenomenon 'language'. It has the following main areas of interest:

phonetics   concerned with the actual sounds used in language, either for their physical properties (*acoustic*), or for the ways in which they are produced by the human organs of speech (*articulatory*);

phonology   concerned with the ways in which the sounds are

7

	organised in languages into systems which convey meaning;
syntax	concerned with the rules underlying sentences, how words are combined to form meaningful sequences; and
semantics	concerned with the nature of meaning in language.

Recent trends show that it is not possible to treat these areas as completely separate from each other. Studies of *discourse* are attempting to investigate the organisation of language in meaningful situations. As a result, increasingly linguists are having to take into account insights deriving from *sociolinguistics* (the study of the ways in which language operates in society) and *psycholinguistics* (the study of psychological issues related to language learning and language use), neither of which has traditionally been regarded as central to linguistics. Obviously, language teachers will not need to be expert in all of these fields, but since teachers are so dependent on insights derived from them an understanding of their basic principles is necessary. Later chapters will look at these areas in more detail.

Language and how we study it

2 How we arrange words in sentences: syntax

As we said in Chapter One, syntax is concerned with the rules underlying sentences and with how words are combined into meaningful sequences. In everyday speech, syntax is perhaps most often referred to as 'grammar', though at one time this term had a wider meaning as the study of all aspects of language. There is a tendency among modern linguists also to use 'grammar' in a more comprehensive sense to refer generally to the knowledge which native speakers have of their language, as well as to the linguist's description of this knowledge.

Words and sentences

There are two general aspects to syntax. One is the structure of *words* and the other is the structure of *sentences*. Both of these may be regarded as basic elements of a language—words because they can combine to form sentences, and sentences because they represent combinations or patterns of words which are systematically put together. But both are essentially arbitrary classifications convenient as units of description for the linguist. Of course, once a writing system has been established for a language, people inevitably make a connection between the concepts 'word' and 'sentence' and the conventional representation and delimitation of these units in writing. But in fact, notwithstanding the claims of certain linguists that words and sentences are 'psychologically real' even to non-literate peoples, there can often be much difficulty in deciding on what to regard as the basic elements when languages are being written down for the first time, as still occasionally happens with remote and hitherto non-literate language communities. It may be very difficult, for example, on the basis of the speech presented by informants, to decide on appropriate boundaries between words, or to discover principles which would justify certain conventions as against others. If we were only now writing English down for the first time, so that we could not appeal to established conventions of writing, what principles would underlie, say, the analysis of the phrase 'these days' as two words, and the analysis of the phrase 'nowadays' as one word (rather than three, perhaps), and what principles would prompt us to assert that neither phrase is a sentence? Such questions can become very much more difficult once one moves outside the Indo-European model of languages and finds examples of lengthy and semantically complex utterances which to the European mind would seem the equivalent of a whole sentence, but which resist analysis as anything but one word. However, it is only when some system for classifying the basic elements of a language has been developed that the study of syntax can proceed to other problems which relate more generally to the way elements combine in structured patterns which are also meaningful sequences. What classes, such as noun and verb, do words fall into, for example, and what are the structural differences between these classes? What rules govern the incidence and ordering of words within sentences and relate structural patterns to communicative categories such as statements, questions and commands?

Linguistic 'rules'

It is worth noting at this point that a linguistic investigation of syntax attempts to provide a description of certain aspects of language as they seem to be—its object is not to lay down rules about how people should speak and write. Linguists, like sociologists, are concerned with the description and classification of behaviour as it actually is. It is true, and we shall return to this question later, that people are sometimes exhorted, notably by parents and teachers, to write and speak 'grammatically' and not to ignore the 'rules of grammar', but within linguistics phrases such as 'rule of grammar' and 'rule of syntax' do not refer to rules set up for people to follow, but to the regularities discovered by linguists to exist in languages. It is a rule of English, for example, that with few exceptions the verb 'do' is used as a support for the main verb in yes/no questions like: 'Did Bill come here yesterday?' On the other hand, this rule does not apply in German, for instance, in which yes/no questions are formulated in accordance with a different principle. In linguistics, then, 'rule' refers to a regular feature of a given language, and is nearer in meaning to 'law' in the scientific sense—the laws of physics, say—than to 'instruction'.

What also follows from this is that all languages and dialects are always described in their own terms on the assumption that they are perfectly satisfactory for the communicative purposes of the people who speak them. If, therefore, we are trying to describe the Cockney dialect, it is appropriate to note and to regard as a rule that the form 'ain't' is used to express the negative of 'am', 'is' and 'are', and it would be quite irrelevant to comment either approvingly or disapprovingly on this form. This principle of accepting languages and dialects as they are for the purposes of description should not however lead to the erroneous assumption sometimes made, and presented as though it were a discovery of linguistic research, that all languages possess, at a given moment, the same expressive power—that is, are all equally effective for all purposes. Some languages are in fact much more satisfactorily developed for particular purposes than are others. It may well be true that all languages have the potential to develop for particular purposes not hitherto considered important by their speakers, but it is certainly not true that all languages have, at the moment, all the vocabulary, even perhaps the structure, to deal with everything and anything in the experience of human beings as a whole. Languages are of course closely tied to the cultures in which they are spoken, and the process of linguistic modification and change, which is essentially the product of cultural change, may take many years.

Having attempted to show the perspective to be adopted for the purpose of describing languages, we will now briefly return to the question of *pre*scription—telling people what they ought to do—as against *de*scription, because some confusion may arise from the fact that many grammars, that is, grammar-books, have been and are designed for instructional purposes and are indeed 'prescriptive grammars' which lay down for learners certain patterns of linguistic behaviour. If we can appreciate that description and prescription have different purposes, then we can see that while prescriptive and descriptive grammars are not to be confused with each other, prescriptive grammars do have a great value in their own right, and they have in fact at certain times been the main vehicle for keeping linguistic study of any kind alive. There is no sense in which a teacher

13

of a language cannot have some idea of a prescriptive grammar, since a teacher who has no idea about how to improve the work of a student cannot claim to be a teacher at all, whether working in the mother tongue or in the foreign language situation. But we must bear in mind that whereas the descriptive linguist is primarily concerned with finding out what people actually do in terms of their linguistic behaviour, anyone constructing a prescriptive grammar is involved in making social judgments about the effect and validity of particular kinds of linguistic behaviour. Teachers of foreign languages in particular arguably have some responsibility for maintaining a socially and widely acceptable 'norm' at least until such time as their students can choose models of foreign language behaviour for themselves. As for the situation in which native speakers criticise other native speakers for 'bad grammar', there may sometimes be a genuine technical and pedagogical issue at stake—ineffectiveness of expression—but just as often the real problem will not be linguistic in any strict sense but will lie in a conflict of social identities, often reflected in patterns of language behaviour.

We have insisted in our discussion so far that linguists attempt to describe things as they actually seem to be, and yet we also said earlier that words and sentences are arbitrary classifications, convenient as units of description for the linguist. How can these two things tie up? The simplest answer, perhaps, is that natural phenomena are not to be confused with the means used to measure and analyse them. The world, for example, is not naturally divided up into yards or metres, but the arbitrary classifications 'yard' and 'metre' allow us to make statements about distances in the world which are meaningful to others who can work with the same system of classification. In the case of speech, we have to say that it is not naturally divided up into words and sentences, but rather into utterances, that is, streams of speech marked off from other utterances by silence at either end. Now it may so happen, of course, that some utterances do coincide with words—e.g. 'Good!'—or with sentences—e.g. 'Thank you for coming'—but for much of the time utterances coincide with neither. Often, for example, there may be no boundaries at all between words in the actual speech-stream—'Lemmedoit!'—'Idonwanna!'—'Whothe-hellyouthinkyouspeakinto?'. Sometimes we leave sentences unfinished, sometimes we produce ungrammatical sentences by changing our minds half-way through about what we want to say, or simply through lapses of memory or attention. We may also make highly elliptical utterances, like 'the blue one', which can only be interpreted by someone aware of the immediate context, and we may, when speaking rapidly, suppress items of structure altogether. To this extent, then, the word and sentence are fictions, descriptive devices used for measuring and analysing language in roughly the same way as degrees centigrade or fahrenheit are fictions, but nevertheless useful for measuring heat. Despite these remarks we have to admit that the adoption of words and sentences as classification-devices in syntax is intuitively appealing, since, whatever utterances speakers of a language may actually produce, they seem to have little difficulty in recognising words as discrete units of speech, and sentences as self-contained combinations of words which display certain regularities, but to what extent this is a result of literacy, we cannot ourselves judge.

Linguists also have to create certain other fictions in order to set up a satisfactory framework for their investigations and to be able to see the wood and not just the trees. For example, groups of people vary from each other in the way they use a particular language, according to their geographical distribution in a country, and often also in accordance with social criteria. And within groups individuals vary in their use of language. In order to make any generalisations at all about a language, as opposed to particular dialects of the language —which, of course, they may also from time to time describe separately—linguists are forced to pretend there is only one version of it. They are also forced to pretend that the rules used by any one individual are consistent, which is unlikely to be true. However, the fact seems to be that native speakers of a language, irrespective of their particular dialects or idiolects, do have a vast amount of shared linguistic knowledge, including tacit awareness of the regularities of their language, so that there would be a high measure of agreement between them with regard to which sequences and combinations could be designated as belonging to the language and which must be rejected as not belonging to the language. In fact the claim must go further than this: it is safe to say that native speakers could never actually produce or hear all the sequences and combinations possible in their language, since these are potentially infinite in number, but in principle would nevertheless, on being presented with any particular one, agree in their judgment as to whether it obeyed the laws of the language or not. In other words, what they would share, certainly to a very significant degree, would be a knowledge of the syntactic rules of the language, and it is these rules, which may be represented as the patterns constituting sentences, which the linguist seeks to describe.

Patterns

To demonstrate what we mean by 'patterns constituting sentences', let us start off by considering the following:

1. Bill hits Fred.
2. It is Bill that hits Fred.
3. Fred is hit by Bill.
4. Does Bill hit Fred?

Presumably all native-speakers of English would agree that the above sequences are permissible in English, and are therefore English sequences, by contrast with, say, 'Hits Bill Fred' or 'Bill hit does Fred?' We will also designate them as sentences of English, since they are structurally complete and integrated sequences by contrast with incomplete sequences like 'Bill hits' and 'hit Fred'. Now we may also argue that all the sentences 1–4 contain the same basic meaning-elements—'Bill', 'hit' and 'Fred'—and, in a sense, present the same basic proposition: 'There is a person called Bill. There is a person called Fred. Bill does something to Fred. What he does is hit him.' Sentence 4, incidentally, also presents this same proposition, though it questions the truth of it, and may do so in a number of ways. And there are other sentences that could reflect this proposition, for example:

5. Bill is hitting Fred.

We could also incorporate our proposition into a larger sentence:

6. That Bill hits Fred is something we all object to.

Or we could attach it to another sentence:

7. We all rejoiced when Bill hit Fred.

We are already beginning to see some basic patterns in the language, and if we understand the meanings of the sentences as opposed to the meanings of the basic elements constituting them, we can appreciate the significance of these patterns in expressing relationships between the elements in the sentences and in presenting the underlying proposition in a number of rather different ways. If we compare sentences 1 and 5, for example, the implication of 1 would usually be that Bill hits Fred habitually, whereas 5 tells us that Bill is hitting Fred at this moment—whether or not he hits him habitually is not stated. There are of course contexts in which 1 might actually mean the same as 5—a boxing commentary, for instance, where 5 would probably be a less acceptable form than 1—but the two forms are by no means always substitutable. Illustrated in these two sentences is a very important syntactic device of English, not shared by all other languages. Both are in the present tense, but they express different *aspects* of the verb 'hit', and though the rules governing aspect are quite complex, English-speakers are highly sensitive to them—'Do you live in London?' could not have the reply: 'Yes, I am owning a house there which I bought two years ago.' Of course, tense in itself is important for locating propositions in time in a more general way:

8. Bill hit Fred (in the past).
9. Bill will hit Fred (in the future).
10. Bill had hit Fred (before something else happened).
11. Bill will have hit Fred (by the time something else happens).

Again, if we recognise the meaning of the sentences, we can appreciate that word-order is very important. 'Bill hits Fred' is quite a different proposition from 'Fred hits Bill', and certainly Fred would be in no doubt about this. Further, we might compare the patterns of sentences 1—Bill hits Fred—and 3—Fred is hit by Bill. As we have said, they both reflect the same proposition, and yet they put it forward differently. Sentence 1 is a neutral or 'normal' statement, in a sense impartial as between Bill and Fred, but sentence 3, in which the *passive* form of the verb is used, puts Fred firmly in the foreground and indicates not just that he is the 'recipient' of Bill's hitting, but emphasises his involvement in the process of being hit. Sentence 3, incidentally, also contains the germ of a further structural pattern—'by Bill' could be deleted altogether, leaving 'Fred is hit' as a perfectly grammatical sentence which might have as an underlying proposition something like: 'Someone (we do not know, or will not say, who) hits Fred', but which at all events focuses on what happens to Fred by omitting mention of who or what causes it to happen to him. Note that sentence 3 is not unlike sentence 2—It is Bill that hits Fred—in that sentence 2 likewise has a specific or emphatic focus—Bill—which is lacking in sentence 1.

In suggesting, in connection with the above examples, that underlying all of them is a basic proposition by virtue of which they may be seen to be related, we have in fact been following a tradition in the study of syntax which finds its clearest and most explicit expression in *transformational generative grammar*, which is by no means the only approach to syntactic analysis, but one which has been extremely influential during the last twenty or so years. In this type of analysis, a distinction is made between *deep-structure*, which is in essence the concept or proposition underlying a sentence, a *surface-structure*, which is the form of words actually used in a particular sentence deriving from an underlying proposition. Mediating between the deep-structure and the surface-structure in this type of grammar is a series of *transformations*, or step-by-step applications of rules. We cannot pretend that there is any longer the same sort of widespread agreement that there once was about the mechanics of the grammar, but according to one version of it, at any rate, our passive sentence 3—Fred is hit by Bill—would derive, via transformation, from a sentence much more like 1—Bill hits Fred. At all events, the deep-structure would be seen in active rather than passive terms, and so to derive the surface-structure of sentence 3, the *passive transformation* would need to be applied, re-arranging the order of the sentence elements 'Bill' and 'Fred', modifying the verb-form and introducing 'by'.

Now the point of this type of analysis is to see how the parts of sentences combine to form varied meanings, to distinguish between sentences systematically and to relate them to other possible sentences with quite different words in them, but constructed in the same or similar ways. Because, by the same token, what we are after ultimately is a set of general rules underlying the syntax of the language and not just a list of sentences with Bill and Fred in them, as in our examples, we should note that Bill and Fred have merely served us as convenience-labels, and we could instead have used symbols like X and Y. In order to discover the scope of a rule, then, a further step would be to see what elements, apart from Bill and Fred, we could put in the X and Y slots. Evidently, there would be vast possibilities—'The man hits Fred', 'The girl hits Fred', 'The door hits Fred', 'Two angry zoo-keepers hit Fred', 'Bill hits the man', 'Bill hits the girl', 'Bill hits the door', 'Bill hits two angry zoo-keepers', 'Two angry zoo-keepers hit the door', 'The girl hits two angry zoo-keepers', and so on and so forth. Actually, we could never exhaust the possibilities if we had to list them all, so we would just have to take enough to formulate a generalisation encompassing all the possibilities, which might turn out to be something like 'X and Y can both be animate or inanimate', but perhaps with certain other qualifications which need not worry us at present. To establish the scope of this sentence-pattern, we could also, staying with the pattern 'X verb Y', try substitutions with the verb, which we would find belongs to a whole class of verbs which we could again encompass in a generalisation, and though it would emerge that there are certain detailed restrictions on the type of sentence-elements which can occur with certain verbs, so that some sub-classification would be necessary, we could in the end derive regularities of wide application. Such regularities, or rules, would then largely account for the fact that though native speakers of English may never before have heard a sentence like 'The flabby slab of cheesecake hit the Martian invader on his ugly snout', they could assign an interpretation to it, and perceive its relation to the equally unlikely but possible sentence 'And the evil Darth Vader was hit by the hail of soft-boiled eggs thrown by Luke Skywalker'. In the course of such investigations it should not be surprising to discover and make explicit regularities of which, though we know them intuitively, we have hitherto had no conscious awareness. Probably all native speakers of English are unconsciously aware, for example, that a sentence like 'Paul has a car', which seems to conform to the X verb Y pattern of 'Bill hits Fred,' has no parallel passive version 'A car is had by Paul'; and yet how many of them could give a list or summarise by descriptive rule those verbs which, like 'hit', are transitive, but cannot be passivised?

People may not, then, actually speak in sentences, but underlying their outward linguistic behaviour is, as far as we can judge, a principled though as yet imperfectly understood system of regularities or patterns. Because this system is shared, certain mutual concessions can be made in actual speech between native speakers of a language, who know how to 'recover' from each other's utterances the regularities which the linguist happens to measure in sentences. That is, we recreate as we listen, the parts of the language system which have been missed out by the speaker.

Morphology

Though we hope to have given some idea of what is involved in the investigation of syntactic patterns, this account of the study of sentences has necessarily been very brief, and there are many complex issues which we cannot raise here. We should, however, devote some discussion to the word, which we have so far neglected. We said earlier that syntax was concerned with the way in which words combine into meaningful sequences, but we now have to add that the word is not in itself the minimal grammatical—or semantic —item in a sentence. If we consider, for instance, two of our earlier examples, sentence 1 and 8—'Bill hits Fred' and 'Bill hit Fred'—we will immediately appreciate that they do not mean exactly the same thing, in the sense that one refers to the present and the other to the past. This difference is signalled to us because in one sentence we see 'hits' and in the other 'hit'. The 's' on the end of 'hit' in sentence 1 is therefore highly significant, even though it is not in itself a word, because it has a semantic function—to indicate 'present time'—and a grammatical one also, as it can only accompany the third person singular of the verb (the 'he', 'she', 'it' form of the verb). The third person singular present tense is in fact signalled in the same way with all English verbs except the modals ('can', 'must', 'will', etc), but we should add, of course, that the 's' we use in writing actually corresponds to three different endings in pronunciation: [s] as in 'sea', [z] as in 'zebra', and [iz] as in 'lizard', and which of these endings occurs depends upon the nature of the preceding sound, e.g. 'hits', 'lends', 'pushes'.

The same endings, governed by the same regularities, are also used to mark the genitive or possessive in English, as in 'Pete's car', 'Bill's bike' and 'Liz's friend'. In these cases, we could say that names like Pete, Bill and Liz each contain one meaning-element which expresses the idea of the person to whom the name refers, but when we add to these names the genitive [s], [z] and [iz], two ideas are then expressed—one the idea of the person, the other the idea 'belonging to this person'. And of course, these endings [s], [z] and [iz] also mark the plural of the vast majority of English nouns. Again, we could say that a noun in the singular, like 'cat', expresses only one fundamental idea, the idea of a cat, but 'cats' expresses two ideas—the idea of 'cat' plus the idea 'more than one'.

Forms of the sort discussed above are referred to as *morphemes*—literally, units of shape—and the behaviour of morphemes, as well as their study, is called *morphology*. Morphemes, which do not have to be endings as in our examples above, are items which cannot be analysed into smaller units which still contain meaning. Some words, then, will in themselves be morphemes — words like 'can', 'do', 'pear', 'lamp', which, though they can be broken down into phonological segments, no longer convey any meaning once they are thus broken down. Other words, however, may be complex words composed of more than one morpheme — words like 'unhappy'—un + happy; 'inapplicable'—in + applic + able; 'colourless' — colour + less; 'odour-free' — odour + free. We have in fact seen two types of morpheme in these complex words. One type, like the 'un' of 'unhappy' and the 'in' of 'inapplicable' is known as a *bound* morpheme because it only occurs in combination with other elements and does not exist as a word on its own. (The 'in' of 'inapplicable', which has the meaning 'not' is of couse different from the preposition 'in' as 'in the house'.) The other type, like the 'less' of 'colourless', and the 'free' of 'odour-free' is known as an *unbound* morpheme, because it can occur as a word in its own right.

To the extent that morphology expresses grammatical relationships, it is of course very important in sentence-structure, and will necessarily be included in any study of syntax. Within a sentence, grammatical patterns have to *agree* with each other, or be in *concord*. For example, we would say 'The child runs down the road' and not 'The child ran down the road', or 'The children are all shouting together' and not 'The children is all shouting together'. This pattern of agreement is part of the grammar of the sentence and in fact we can see that the basic meaning-elements which make up words may be grammatical forms or may be forms which carry the fundamental content of the sentence. Actually, among words themselves we can see that some are 'content words', carrying what we might term the grammatically unpredictable semantic load of the sentence, and others are more in the nature of 'function words' or grammatical tools. In the sentence 'Bill is hitting Fred', for example, we may well, and quite unpredictably, substitute any number of other content words for 'Bill'—Pete, Jim, Arthur, the butcher, the baker, etc.—and thereby change the identity of the culprit, but if we wish to maintain the same tense and aspect expressed in the original sentence, we cannot, given this particular sentence-pattern, change the forms 'is' and '—ing', which are absolute requirements of the grammar, predictable from the grammar, and therefore in some sense part of the grammar. Morphology, then, interacts with other aspects of grammar, but it does so happen that English has very little agreement morphology indeed, and what it does have is largely communicatively redundant. The price of this is that it has instead a comparatively rigid word-order, whereas languages richer in agreement morphology, like German, can afford a greater range of possibilities for word-order on the basis that morphology will still point out grammatical relationships when normal word-order is modified.

Let us just return briefly to our earlier example, 'hits' versus 'hit'. Now we could have said about the sentences concerned—'Bill hits Fred' and 'Bill hit Fred'—that they contained different words, analysing both 'hits' and 'hit' as words in their own right. In retrospect, however, it should be evident that if we were to proceed in this way, we would in the end have to list every word-form in the language as a separate word. This would be extremely uneconomical considering that, as we have seen, morphemic analysis enables us to discover that the structure of sentences, can be summarised to a large extent by rules if we accept that words have a 'basic form' and morphological variants. And it would seem that a tacit knowlege of the regularities of word-structure is indeed part of the native speaker's general knowledge of syntax—most native speakers of English would have no difficulty in supplying regular plural forms for such words as 'thracket', 'bodog', 'grangua' or 'flemitch', none of which they are likely to have seen before.

Grammar and use
Naturally, interpretations of what people say cannot be made solely on the basis of grammar. Syntax must be seen as interacting with semantics and phonology, and also other things which lie outside linguistics, like knowledge of the world and of people, in the expression and communication of meaning. What is clear, however, is that any utterance produced in English or in any other language must by and large reflect the regularities contained in syntax if its meaning is to be understood; and if we are to understand how language functions as a total system, then we need to investigate and describe the rules of syntax. While giving us some insight into the nature of language, however, a description cannot predict for us how people will actually use language in practice. And again, many grammatical sentences which the rules may potentially allow will never be produced. It would be perfectly possible, for example, to produce a grammatical sentence running in writing to 300 pages or in speech to 24 hours or indeed to the end of time—perhaps a sentence of the sort 'And I tell you again and again and again and again and again and again and again and again and again and again and again and again and again . . . etc.' There can be no grammatical rule saying where a sentence should stop, so such a sentence would

have to be classed as grammatical though also, to most people presumably, as unacceptable. Further, linguists cannot legislate for tact, lies or hypocrisy. A case in which someone says 'How nice to see you' when what they really mean is 'How did I manage to have the bad luck to bump into you?' is a matter for the philosopher rather than the linguist. The field of syntax is, then, hedged about with many abstractions and idealisations, and for methodological reasons must be. But the contribution of the study of syntax is only one contribution, though a fascinating one, to the study of language, and must be put together with the contributions from the other branches of linguistics for its value to be fully appreciated.

In the past, grammar has occupied a central position in language teaching and language learning, and indeed it is still extremely important because a very limited set of rules will produce a range of sentence-patterns into which we can fit many thousands of content words to express an enormous variety of meanings. For the foreign language teacher dealing with students of homogeneous mother tongue a knowledge of *contrastive syntax*—that is, a knowledge of how syntactic patterns vary as between the mother tongue and the foreign language—is of very great value in guiding the choice of materials and determining appropriate remedial work. Even the foreign language teacher dealing with students of various mother tongues should at least try to find out the really salient points of contrast in order to be able to understand some of the difficulties students experience with grammar, since *interference* (see Chapter Eleven) is a common phenomenon among learners, and it is always useful to know where difficulties are likely to lie. However, simply to be able to produce grammatical sentences of the language can never be enough: we have to learn both to use grammatical sentences naturally and easily and to use them according to the conventions of normal speech and normal writing, and as language teachers we must be concerned with grammar in effective use.

3 The sounds of the language: phonology

Phonology and phonetics are both concerned with the sounds of languages. As stated in Chapter One, phonology is concerned with the ways in which the sounds are organised in languages into systems which convey meaning—in conjunction with the syntactic and semantic systems—while phonetics is concerned with the actual sounds used in language, either for their physical properties or for the ways in which they are produced by the organs of speech. Though the focus of these studies is somewhat different, they are complementary, each providing the other with information and clues for further investigations.

To say that phonology is concerned with sounds organised into systems for conveying meaning, while phonetics is concerned with actual speech sounds, may appear strange; if phonetics is concerned with actual speech sounds, this implies that the sounds with which phonology is concerned are not actual speech sounds. In essence, this is so. But how can a sound not be an actual speech sound? The answer has to do with the difference between speech as we hear it and articulate it, and speech as we interpret it and mean it.

If we consider speech in purely physical terms, what we are forced to say about it is that it is a stream of noise produced by the articulatory organs, varied by pauses and changes in pitch, volume and type of sound. This is in fact the way in which languages strike us when we do not understand them at all. What we have learnt in the case of languages we do understand, however, is how to analyse the stream of speech noise, picking out from it those features which are important for meaning, and ignoring those which are not. In addition to identifying the basic sound distinctions, such as *p*, *m* and *b*, we also, of course, understand the conventions by which the languages we know allow sounds to be combined with other sounds to form units of meaning such as *pet*, *met* and *bet*. By the same token, we are aware of the combinations not permitted—for example, *trg* could not be a word by the conventions of English (but is a word in Slovenian). And there are of course other features in the stream of speech noise such as stress (emphasis), volume and pauses, all of which can have significant consequences for meaning, and all of which speakers of a language can recognise and interpret. Now, so far this may seem straightforward, and in a sense it would be if all speakers of a certain language all unerringly produced exactly the same sounds in the same places; but this is not the case. For one thing, instead of producing all sounds clearly, people often only make a movement or gesture towards them. For another, objective studies can show that people do not produce the same sounds as other people even when they think they are doing so. There are many differences between the sounds produced by adults and those produced by children, for example. In fact, it is doubtful whether even the same person can produce exactly the same sound several times in succession. And again, once one begins to combine sounds with others to form words, what one supposes to be the same sound occurring in different words and in different places may not be the same sound at all—consider the *v* of *very* as against the *v* of *have* in the phrase 'I have to go now'. One may well perceive a *v* in the *have*, but the chances are that what was actually said was more like 'I hafto . . .'. So with speech sounds, there is a difference between reality—the actual, physical noises of speech—and perception—the way in which the actual speech-signal is interpreted.

An analogy might help to clarify some aspects of the difference between reality and perception with regard to speech sounds. We are all used to reading many different styles of handwriting, so that if we asked ten people each to copy out in longhand the same passage from the same book, it would not surprise us to find that while we could in each case read the result well enough to judge that the same passage had indeed been copied by all ten writers, each style of handwriting differed from the others in size, formation of the characters and angle of writing. So what we are in effect doing when we read someone's writing is conducting a comparison between the actual written characters and a generalised form of the characters of which we have a mental picture. So long as the characters of the script stand in a predictable relationship to the generalised forms, comprehension is possible. Roughly the same situation applies to the sounds of speech. The speaker of a language is aware of the sounds of the language as they are ideally, and actual speech sounds are interpreted by projection onto these ideal sounds which form the system for keeping meanings apart in the language. It is by virtue of this mechanism that the actual speech sounds produced by different speakers of a language and the speech sounds produced by speakers of different dialects of a language can be equated to the same system. Phonology, then, is concerned with this system of 'ideal' sounds which keep meanings apart, and phonetics with the sounds people actually utter. But of course it is only by investigating the actual sounds of speech that we can begin to gain a picture of the sound-distinctions important in the system for conveying meaning, so that in practice linguists approach the phonology of a language through a prior study of the actual speech sounds. We shall also first consider here how actual speech sounds are produced and described.

Describing sounds
Traditionally, phoneticians divide speech sounds between *consonants* and *vowels*. The division is not absolutely straightforward, but in general terms it is made according to the way sounds are produced or, in the terminology of phonetics, 'articulated'.

To start with the vowels, these are articulated with the mouth relatively unobstructed, so as to allow passage of an airstream from the lungs straight through the mouth to the outside. However, on the way up from the lungs, the airstream passes through the vocal cords, which are two pieces of firm, elastic tissue spanning the windpipe in the larynx (or 'Adam's Apple') and the vocal cords vibrate extremely rapidly, closing together, then opening again. This happens many times during the production of a vowel, and the effect of each closure, which dams the airstream from the lungs, is to build up additional pressure below the vocal cords, so that when they open again, air is pushed through them in a sort of miniature explosion. Because the opening and closing is so rapid, what is heard coming from the mouth is perceived as a continuous stream of sound. Precisely what sound is formed, however, depends on the shape of the mouth-cavity and the resonances produced in it, and this shape depends on how open the mouth is and on the position of the tongue, which can of course be moved upwards, downwards, forwards, backwards and sideways. For example, if you say 'car-key' [ka:ki:], you should notice that in producing the [a:] of 'car' [ka:], your tongue is relatively flat in your mouth, though raised somewhat at the back, whereas with the [i:], the tongue is generally higher in the mouth, with the front part raised higher than the rest. The presence or absence of lip-rounding can also be crucial for distinguishing meaning in some languages, such as French and German, but though it usually occurs to some degree in the pronunciation of certain English sounds, it is of no consequence for meaning in English. Again, English has no nasal vowels, as do French and Portuguese. A nasal vowel is produced by leaving the nasal cavity open during the articulation of a vowel, with the effect of adding to the articulatory system a secondary resonating chamber to supplement the mouth. The difference between an oral (mouth-only) vowel and a nasal vowel can be heard if one first says 'da' as in 'dad', and then makes a deliberate effort to keep the nose open while pronouncing the same sound. The result should be something like the French word *dans* (dã). It must also be mentioned that many languages observe a distinction between monophthongs and diphthongs. The former are sometimes called 'pure' vowels, and are perceived as being articulated with the tongue held in one position throughout. In terms of its Greek origins, the name of the latter implies that they are 'twice-sounded' vowels, though actually they contain a continuum of different sounds produced by movement of the tongue in the mouth during articulation. An example of a diphthong would be the (ai) sound (like 'eye') in words such as *fine* and *mine*. In practice, probably most if not all vowels are articulated as diphthongs, even though not perceived as such, because in rapid speech the tongue is on the move the whole time.

What distinguishes the articulation of the consonants from that of the vowels is the relative occlusion, or closing, of the mouth or the mouth and the nasal cavity. Those consonants whose articulation involves complete occlusion of the mouth are usually called *stops*. An example is the *p* of *pie* or *pen*. The sound of the consonant is produced in this case on the release of the occlusion, as a result of which air-pressure has built up behind it. Stops can be *voiced*, that is, the vocal cords can be vibrating, as with vowels, or *voiceless*, that is, the vocal cords are at rest during the articulation of the sound. The sound (p) is a voiceless stop, but (b) as in *bread* or *board* is a voiced stop. English has three pairs of oral stops—p/b; t/d; k/g—each pair

consisting of sounds which are distinguished from each other only by
the absence of voice in the one case and its presence in the other.
Similar to the stops in that the mouth is occluded are the nasals like [m]
and [n]. However, while the mouth remains occluded during their
production, air escapes through the nose, causing resonance in the
nasal cavity. Another type of consonant is the *fricative*, which differs
from the stop in that occlusion is almost but not quite complete.
Sounds like [f] and [v] are fricatives, in this case formed by close
approximation of the lower lip and the upper front teeth. Like stops,
fricatives can be voiced or voiceless and in our example [f] is voiceless
and [v] voiced. The high-pitched fricatives such as [s] and [z] form a
sub-class called *sibilants*. Like other fricatives, they are continuous
sounds, with air escaping from the mouth throughout their articulation. A further class of consonants is that of the *affricates*, which are
essentially combinations of stop and fricative. They can be heard in
words like *church* and *judge*. However, the *ch* [tš] and *j* [dž] sounds in
such words are not usually perceived as consisting of two components. Like stops, fricatives and sibilants, affricates can be voiced or
voiceless. Yet another class of consonant is the *lateral*, exemplified in
English by [l], where the tongue blocks off the centre of the mouth, but
allows the airstream to flow around both sides of it. In English, there
are some consonants which cannot be placed in the above categories
and cause problems of description. [r], for example, often behaves
more like a vowel than a consonant, though traditionally classified as
a consonant. [h] is sometimes designated a 'cavity-fricative' because
its articulation, like that of fricatives, involves air-turbulence, but this
is not restricted to any particular place in the oral cavity. It is also a
'characterless' sound, gaining its quality from the vowel following it.
[w] and [j]—the latter standing for the y-sound of *yacht*—are
sometimes described as semi-vowels, since in their articulation they
are more vowel-like than consonant-like; on the other hand, they
sometimes function more like consonants.

The way speech sounds are described will depend on who is
describing them and for what purpose. The acoustic phonetician, for
example, will describe them in terms of their physical properties as
sound waves. Generally, though, sounds are described by reference to
their articulation.

In the case of consonants, the criteria used for description are (1) the
place where a sound is articulated and (2) the manner in which it is
articulated. Neither criterion will suffice on its own, since different

sounds can be articulated in the same place but in different ways, just as different sounds can be articulated in the same way but in different places. For British English, the descriptions applied to sounds according to the *place* where they are articulated are broadly as follows: *bilabial* (referring to sounds made with both lips, e.g. [p], [m], [b] as in *pet, met, bet*); *labio-dental* (referring to sounds formed with the lower lip and upper front teeth, e.g. [f] and [v] as in *fire* and *very*); *dental* (referring to sounds formed with the tip or blade of the tongue placed against the back of the upper front teeth, e.g. *th* [θ] as in *thin* and *th* [ð] as in *this*); *aveolar* (referring to the sounds formed with the tongue tip or blade placed against the alveolar ridge, the hard ridge just behind the upper front teeth—e.g. [t], [n], as in *ten, nine*); *palato-alveolar* (referring to a position slightly behind the alveolar ridge against which the tongue is placed—e.g. for *sh* [š] as in *she* and *shy*); *velar* (referring to sounds formed with the back of the tongue contacting the soft palate—e.g. [k] as in *car*, [g] as in *gag*, *ng* [ŋ] as in *sing*). A full description of the *manner* of articulation would require reference to three criteria: whether or not the vocal cords are vibrating during the production of a sound, that is, whether it is *voiced* or *voiceless*; whether or not the nasal cavity is open or closed, that is whether a sound is *nasal* (nasal cavity open) or *oral* (nasal cavity closed, mouth only open); what sort of a sound is involved from an articulatory point of view. In discussing the articulation of sounds we have already come across many of the relevant categories —*stop, fricative, sibilant, affricate, lateral* etc. Putting all these criteria together, then, we would be able to describe the initial sound of *sing*, for example, as a *voiceless, alveolar, central, oral sibilant*, or the *ng* [ŋ] sound of *sing* as a *voiced, velar, central, nasal* consonant.

The description of vowels is achieved in a different manner, partly because articulation is not so closely associated with one particular part of the mouth as it is for consonants, partly because it is useless to talk about different manners of articulation where vowels are concerned. The convention used is to divide the mouth up into different locations, and to indicate the vowels in terms of these locations by reference to the highest point of the tongue during articulation. This 'mapping' of the vowels in the mouth is usually shown in the form of a stylised 'vowel diagram' representing a sideways view of the inside of the mouth. The vowels of a language can then be placed inside this diagram, and a linguist can then deduce from it the vowel-system of the language. We show below the vowel-diagram for British English (monophthongs only).

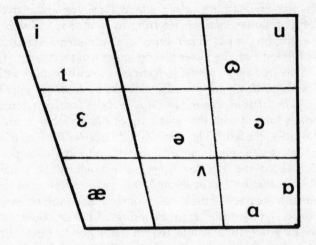

This 'mapping system' is certainly not an exact measuring device. Its weakness is that only someone highly familiar with the system already can assign really accurate values to the vowels shown, since the divisions are arbitrary. On the other hand, precise measurements cannot be used in this sort of description, which is concerned with bringing out *perceived* contrasts between vowels. It is these contrasts which are important, not exact measurements. At the same time, it is possible to describe the articulation of particular vowels in greater detail by stating whether they are *oral* or *nasal*, by giving information about their *relative length* (short, half-long or long, as in *bit*, *bead*, *beat*) and by saying whether they are *tense* or *lax*. This last criterion is traditionally associated with the amount of muscular energy required in the articulation of a vowel. The vowel of *seat*, for example, is tense, while that of *sit* is lax. In general, tense vowels tend to be longer than lax vowels.

The sound system
Now we have given some information about the articulation and description of speech sounds, we can return to the question of the difference between the system of 'ideal' sounds which keep meanings

apart, and the actual sounds of speech. For more than a hundred years now the term *phoneme* has been used to designate a sound belonging to the set of 'significant sounds' which form the system for conveying meaning. In recent years, some linguists have contested the necessity for the notion of the phoneme, but it is nevertheless a convenient idea. By contrast with the phoneme, an actual speech-sound produced by a speaker is often referred to as a *phone*. From what was said earlier about the variety of actual speech-sounds which can be equated to the same system of sound-distinctions rather in the way that different handwritings can be equated to the same generalised forms of written symbols, it should follow that the set of phones in a language is greater than the set of phonemes. Just as many noticeably differing handwritten versions of, say, 't' all represent 't', so several noticeably differing phones can all represent the same phoneme. If we think, for example, about the possible pronunciations of the word *city* and concentrate on the sound represented by the third letter in it, we will probably recall at least three pronunciations we have heard: one in which this sound really is like a 't' sound, one in which the word sounds as a whole like 'ci'y', where the third sound is really a non-sound—actually a glottal stop, with momentary cutting off of the airstream in the throat—and one in which the word sounds rather like 'cidy'. This last pronunciation is more typical of American English, but can be heard in British English too. Now it is very unlikely that any speaker of British English, at any rate, would fail to understand the word in context, whichever one of the three pronunciations mentioned was used. So what happens here is that three phones are all equated to one phoneme, the phoneme /t/. The technical term for these alternative actual sounds all representing the same phoneme is *allophones*, and we can say on the basis of our 'city' example that the phoneme /t/ has at least three allophones or allophonic variations. Sometimes allophones are used randomly, sometimes they are conditioned by dialect, and sometimes they are conditioned by the sounds occurring around them. We saw in our earlier 'I hafto . . .' example that the phoneme /v/ has an allophone [f] before a voiceless [t]. Speed of articulation also affects allophonic variation.

If a language abounds in phones, how does one establish what the phonemes are, and what the relationship is between allophones and phonemes? This can only be done by referring to meaning. In practice, 'meaning tests' are carried out by comparing sound-sequences differing from each other in a minimal way. When differences of sound make differences of meaning, as in *pet* versus *bet*, then we conclude that different phonemes are involved. Variations on a sound which make no difference to meaning would be classed as allophones. But isolating the sounds of a language and arranging them as phones and phonemes is only the beginning of descriptive work. Another part of the task is to see how sounds can be combined, and here languages vary in their conventions. German, for example, permits combinations like [p] + [f], as in *Pfropfen*, whereas English does not.

What ultimately distinguishes the phonetician's task from that of the phonologist is that while the phonetician will wish to be as exhaustive as possible in his description of speech sounds, the phonologist will wish to concentrate on the *distinctive features* of sounds—those features which serve to distinguish meaning. While it is therefore of interest to the phonetician that in English the p-sound in the word *pin* is aspirated, that is, followed by a sharp puff of breath, while the p-sound in the word *spin* is not aspirated, the phonologist can for his own purposes ignore this phenomenon, since aspiration has, in English, no signficance at all in conveying meaning. On the other hand, features such as *voiceless*, *labial* and *stop* are a different case altogther—changing any one of these features within a sound is almost certain to affect meaning. Of course, the fact that having isolated the phonemes of a language one can then go on to analyse the distinctive features in the sound-system means that phonemes are not after all the minimal units of sound conveying meaning in the language. But they are a convenient notion, a sort of shorthand for particular combinations of distinctive features.

Combining sounds

We have so far been concerned with those sounds which we perceive as the basic sound distinctions necessary to convey meaning. We might like to consider these sounds, which we can combine together to form speech-sequences, as the 'alphabet' for speech, since there is a certain parallel between such sounds and the letters of the written alphabet. But of course the total 'sound-effect' of a speech sequence is not produced simply by adding and combining phones together. Human beings do not normally speak in flat monotones. Their speech has special contours which contribute to the conveying of meaning and to the conveying of attitude. The two major elements making up speech contours are usually referred to as *stress* and *intonation*. Stress refers to the emphasis placed in a speech sequence on certain elements in it—syllables, words or phrases—in relation to others. In English, stress operates at two levels—as *word-stress* and *syntactic stress*. Differences in word-stress can be perceived by comparing certain noun/verb pairs like 'the *con*tract' versus 'to con*tract*'. In this case, the main stress falls on the first syllable of the noun and the second syllable of the verb. Perhaps the most crucial aspect of word-stress in English is that syllables other than the syllable bearing the main stress tend to be articulated rather weakly by comparison, and vowels other than the vowel-bearing main stress tend to be reduced towards an 'i' sound, as in the word 'in', or an 'eh' sound. There is an old joke about English having only one vowel— the vowel 'eh'. In one way or the other, then, failure to master the word-stress system of English will mean failure to comprehend, especially as articles and prepositions have varying stress, depending on their position and syntactic function. Syntactic stress supplies the dominant stress for the whole of an utterance, and the major stress or stresses will be placed on those parts of the utterance to which the speaker wishes to give most prominence. This part or these parts will often be the 'new information', or the least predictable element, in the speaker's message. If we consider a statement like 'I've just bought a new pullover for two pounds', it would be possible to give main stress to any of the content-words or sense-groups in it. This can be demonstrated by using the sentence or variants of it as an answer to questions like: 'Who's just bought a new pullover?' ('*I've* just bought a new pullover . . .') 'You bought a new pillow?' ('No, I've bought a new *pullover* . . .') 'You bought a used pullover?' ('No, I've bought a *new* pullover . . .') and so on. Syntactic stress also encompasses contrastive stress: 'It was *Peter* who caught chicken-pox' (not *Bill*). Syntactic stress can only be fully predicted in relation to given communication situations. It is, however, a very important characteristic of English, since English can use stress alone to make contrasts which in some other languages require the use of additional words.

If stress supplies the rhythm of speech, intonation supplies the tunes. It is a crucial element in speech because very often it is the only linguistic sign of a speaker's intentions. For example, we are not always obliged to use question word-order for asking questions, particularly questions checking whether we have understood something correctly. In speech the only thing separating the statement 'He's coming to the party' from the question 'He's coming to the party?' is the difference between the falling intonation for the statement and the rising intonation for the question. However, it is actually far more complex than this—only the intonation patterns will tell us whether the question is a neutral, innocent one, an angry one, a shocked one, a malevolent one, and so on. Intonation, then, is a marker of attitudes, and though the information we derive from it is not in itself linguistic, it is information vital for 'survival' in communication situations. The problem with stress and intonation is that the conventions are not universal: they have to be studied carefully in relation to each language. Learning the basic sound distinctions of a language may not be easy, but it is relatively straightforward. To learn speech contours, we have to learn the culture, and in some sense psychology too, both individual and collective.

4 How we study meaning: semantics

In many ways, semantics is the most difficult aspect of linguistics to describe simply. It is concerned with the relationship between meaning and language, but there are so many ways of looking at this problem that it is always difficult to establish clear, scientific procedures. Some people consider semantics to be properly the concern of philosophers rather than linguists, and psychologists have a claim to make as well. Certainly it will make a difference to what extent we want to relate problems of meaning to thinking, or communication, or behaviour.

There are also difficulties with semantics which do not occur so much with phonology and syntax. Native-speakers may often disagree (as many law-suits indicate) over exactly what is meant by a particular piece of language, either spoken or written, and there is no clear-cut procedure for establishing unambiguously the meaning of a text or utterance. Yet at the same time it is possible to make *some* generalisations about meaning: even if we do not always know exactly what a particular text means, we certainly know that there are some things that it cannot mean. At the same time, our interpretation of any text works in a number of different ways, which should be distinguished.

First, and most important, any utterance in isolation carries some sort of meaning: there is a basic sense to it. If I write *the fish*, you will know that I am not referring to a tree or a cabbage. Even if I write *the land-fish*, you will be able to make some sort of guess about what I mean, while possibly thinking that it sounds rather nonsensical. It may be nonsensical, but it is not completely meaningless, as it would be if I wrote *the strindle*, or some other unknown word. Furthermore, if I write *the fish is in the sea*, you will know what I am talking about, even though you may think that it is a rather uninteresting thing to say, and may wonder which particular fish I am referring to. Even if I simply write *yes*, you can at once contrast it meaningfully with *no*, and in some sense limit its meaning, although *yes* conveys very little to a reader unless there is a context to fit it into. Meaning of this kind is that which will normally be communicated by dictionaries or straightforward accounts of the grammatical forms of English. It is fundamental, but it is by no means the whole of meaning.

Since meaning links language with messages, and messages are usually about things in the world, independent of language, we also react to the things themselves which are being referred to. *Lion* may conjure up associations with real lions, or with symbolic lions, as in heraldry, with all the possible patriotic associations of the British lion, the Lion of Judah, and so on. Each community will have particular associations for particular things in the real world, and these will be reflected in the meanings within that community. Some terms will have very strong emotional content; consider the implications of terms of kinship: *motherland*, or *fatherland*, the use of *brothers* by members of religious or political groups, and so on.

Language carries other kinds of messages also, however. We will, for example, recognise various stylistic features which indicate the probable situation in which a word is used. A *letter* may be an *epistle* in certain religious contexts, a *dispatch* for a newspaper correspondent, a *communication* in business circles, and a *missive* as a joke among schoolboys trying to use archaic language. Such stylistic features may identify particular dialects, dates, topics, and levels of formality. They will also show whether something is probably spoken or written, part of a monologue or a conversation, whether the user is telling a joke, starting a lecture, or writing a formal speech. They may also, of course, indicate the style of particular authors or speakers.

Beyond this, the language used will also convey as part of the message, indications of the feelings and attitudes of the speaker/writer. All these features are interpreted by anyone who receives a message, by means of the total organisation of the message, its form and its content.

Sense and reference
Semantics, then, must ultimately account for our understanding of all these aspects of language. The main problem is how to limit the

potentially vast area which is opened up, so that it becomes manageable. And at the beginning it is helpful to distinguish between problems of *reference*, of how the language refers to the non-linguistic world, and problems of *sense*, of how the elements of the language and their meanings relate to each other. The latter area is a great deal easier to describe than the former, and is concerned mainly, but not solely, with the relationships between the words of the language.

Such relationships are of course very important to us, for when we define terms we usually define them in relation to other terms in the language: a dictionary does this all the time. To illustrate what is meant here, let us consider some of the most basic sense relations in English. Below is listed a number of pairs of words, and each of these pairs expresses a different kind of semantic relationship.

cow – bull	husband – wife
mile – yard	thin – fat
lend – borrow	yesterday – tomorrow

In each of these examples a different sort of relationship is expressed, and it is possible to think of other pairs which express the same relationship. *Cow* and *bull* share the same features except that the former is female and the latter is male. *Husband* and *wife* show features frequently found in expressions of relationships: they are reciprocal terms, so that if I say 'She is my wife', it would normally also be true to say 'I am her husband'. A *mile* is a measure which includes a *yard*: the relationship is one of inclusion (but compare *mile* with *kilometre*). *Thin* is the opposite of *fat*. If I *lend* you something, you must be *borrow*ing it from me, just as if I *sell* you something you must be *buy*ing it from me. *Yesterday* expresses a time relationship in relation to the past which *tomorrow* expresses in relation to the future.

From relationships such as these, it is possible to show why some sentences will not be acceptable in normal English. None of the following sentences would be acceptable, for example, although we cannot strictly say that they are ungrammatical:

That bull is this calf's mother.
She is my wife but I am not her husband.
There are twelve miles in a yard.
This extremely thin man is extraordinarily fat.
I didn't borrow his book; he just lent it to me.

I will help you yesterday.

It is true that it is sometimes possible to make some sort of sense out of sentences of this type (*He is a very thin fat man*, for example), but we only make sense of them by recognising the limitations of meaning relationships, and reinterpreting the possibilities in the light of the sentence we have heard. Notice also that all the examples we have cited do give rise to problems of usage when we try to interpret their relations strictly. We can say, for example, that *bull* and *cow* share all features except sex, so that we can draw up a table as follows:

	bull	*cow*
animate	+	+
mammal	+	+
human	−	−
cattle	+	+
female	−	+

We can list any features which we consider relevant and indicate which are shared and which are not, but in practice we must be clear about the status of the terms we are discussing. In the speech of many urban English-users *cow* is a general term in the way *bull* is not. To look down from the top of a hill and remark 'Those are cows' without deliberately excluding bulls is permissible; to remark 'Those are bulls' without excluding cows is not accepted. So *cow* may contrast with *bull* by being '+ female', but in general usage may be + or − female. Thus although clear-cut analyses of this kind do have value, there are nearly always problems in defining the exact nature of the usage before an unambiguous analysis can be attempted.

Nonetheless, by examining the meanings of words in this way, the linguist is able to determine some of the ways in which a particular language categorises the features of the world which are found significant in a particular culture. We recognise that categories like sex, time, kinship, distance are significant in the culture, and we may of course discover that particular concepts and categorisations are found in all languages. However, it is frequently found that the significance of particular categories, and the ways in which they are expressed, varies considerably from language to language. The extent to which linguistic categories overlap with those categories accepted by particular cultural groups is a matter of constant debate among linguists and anthropologists. And this takes us back to the question with which we opened this section, for the relationship between linguistic meaning and the real world is a matter of reference rather than sense relations.

Problems of reference

The study of reference has traditionally been the concern of the philosopher rather than the linguist. Such a study has a long and complicated history, and there are many different ways of considering problems of meaning. It is possible, for example, to think about meaning in relation to processes of thinking, and to try to relate the sense relations discussed above to logical processes. It is also possible to consider the problem as one of understanding communication, seeing language as a device for communicating information, or as one of understanding human behaviour, seeing language as a means of doing things, being concerned not so much with the messages themselves as with how sense relations are used in the real world to achieve practical results. As will be seen later, in Chapter Fourteen, the attitude we take to problems of reference may have a direct influence on our approach to syllabus design, and to a definition of what it means to 'learn' a language.

Context and meaning

So far, we have referred to sense relations for individual words, but we have not related this to the contexts in which they occur. It is possible to make some predictions about what words will occur together in a particular language. English textbooks in English schools used to ask pupils to learn some of the most striking collocations (words which collocate are ones which customarily occur together). Thus lists like *flock of sheep*, *pride of lions*, *swarm of bees*, were learnt by heart. Essentially what was being learnt was a highly specialised word for a *collection* of living creatures. Similarly, we discover that persons performing more or less identical tasks are called *referees* in football and *umpires* in cricket or tennis. A football match may be scored three-*nil*, but a game played with a racket will be scored three-*love*. A great deal of learning foreign languages involves acquiring the ability to avoid inappropriate collocations. We also have to recognise some collocations which have become so fixed that they can scarcely be broken at all. Idioms, while they vary in the extent to which their meaning can be worked out from the combined meanings of their parts, are usually collections of words which function as if they are single words. These vary from possibly quite lengthy proverbial sayings like 'A bird in the hand is worth two in the bush' to phrasal verbs like *turn in*, meaning *go to bed*. Neither of these examples can be broken down into smaller units without the meaning being shattered, whereas *turn* in *turn round* can be separated without losing its meaning. The whole area of how we use quotation, reference and allusion in ordinary language has been very little explored, but it is clear that meaning is expressed frequently through collections of words which mean a great deal more than the sum of their parts.

Even if we accept that both words and groups of words possess meaning in some abstract sense, it is clear that that is not the total picture of sense relations in language. Words relate to each other in sentences, and the grammar of the language carries meaning as well as the vocabulary. For example, if I want to express the idea of future action in English, I may do this by using a word which always carries future meaning, like *tomorrow* which we referred to above, or by using the verb *will*. There is no fixed morpheme for expressing futurity in English (which is why it is sometimes said that there is no future tense in English). On the other hand we have a systematic procedure for changing the verb form to express the past, using — with most verbs—the form *-ed*, as in *He worked for two hours*. Notice that you can say *He will work for two hours tomorrow*, or *He works for two hours tomorrow*, or *He is going to work . . .* or *He is working . . .*, but you do not have the same freedom of manoeuvre with *yesterday*, with which you must retain the past tense form, *He worked for two hours yesterday*. But the grammatical form, the past morpheme *-ed*, carries meaning which overlaps in some way with one of the features of *yesterday*. Yet we cannot say that *-ed* necessarily involves a past meaning. It does not in the sentence *If you worked hard you would succeed in your exams*, for example. Nor are grammatical categories necessarily the same as semantic categories. *Une victime* in French may well be a man, even though the word is marked as feminine. *I have got some trousers on* does not imply that I am wearing several pairs, and *I am working* may refer to either today or tomorrow, as we saw.

But we cannot deduce the meaning of a sentence simply from seeing the various meanings of the content words in it. The grammar of the language enables us to express relations between the meanings enclosed by the content words. In the sentence *Julius Caesar left his toga at the baths* we understand from *left* that the action (or inaction)

40

took place in the past, from *his* that the toga belonged to Julius Caesar, from *at* where it happened, and from *the* that the baths was an identifiable place and that the speaker assumes that there is no further necessary information to help the hearer to identify *baths* adequately for understanding of the message. All these features are essential elements in enabling us to understand the message.

There are further elements of context which we interpret in understanding language. We follow links between sentences and paragraphs, for example by recognising the force of words like *therefore*, *however*, and *thus*. We recognise the structure of particular utterances by responding to *in conclusion* and other verbal comments on the linguistic situation made by speakers. There is a whole range of devices by which meaning is referred backwards and forwards throughout an extended piece of language. The pronoun system is one of the ways in which we are able to refer either forward ('When *she* arrived, the *duchess* bought a balloon') or back ('The *duchess* bought a balloon when *she* arrived'). But one pronoun takes us out of language altogether into the wider, social context. If we say *I* we mean, of course, 'the speaker', but this will only be interpretable if it is known who, or at least what sort of person, is speaking. To some extent any use of language becomes only fully meaningful when it is related to a situation: *Which* baths did Julius Caesar leave his toga at? But this sort of contact with the real world cannot be described in a linguistic theory, for it depends entirely on the shared knowledge of the participants in the speech event. Semantic studies must restrict themselves to the systems through which meaning is conveyed. Even within this restriction, as this chapter has indicated, there are a number of different questions to consider, none of which can be answered very tidily.

5 Language in society: sociolinguistics

Linguistic studies, as we have seen, often concern themselves with language as an (idealised) system, isolated from problems of use. In the last two decades, however, even traditional linguistic studies have had to take notice of how languages are used. This is partly because the more we study problems of meaning, the more we are forced to consider the situations which impose meaning on the linguistic system, and partly because sociological studies themselves have become increasingly helpful in what they have to say about language use in society. Nonetheless, it is helpful to distinguish between sociolinguistics proper and what has been called the sociology of language. The former is concerned with producing adequate descriptions of language, recognising that no adequate description can ignore the ways in which language is used in interaction between speakers and hearers, writers and readers. The latter is a broader and more diffuse study for it demands that insights from disciplines such as sociology, social psychology and anthropology be integrated with insights from core linguistics to provide an account of how language is used in social life. It is clear that both forms of study are important sources for teachers, for language is the most important of the systems by which knowledge, beliefs and attitudes are passed on from one generation to the next. At the same time, the same factors which make such studies important make them immensely difficult as well, for language operates in so many complex ways, and is so closely bound up with our thought processes and our overt behaviour, that it is difficult to separate one aspect from another distinctly enough to be able to make clearly defined statements.

42

It is possible, however, to make a number of observations about language and language use which are both verifiable and which contradict many of our implicit beliefs. This chapter will introduce and discuss the most important ideas deriving from sociolinguistic studies, and will also try to describe some of the major theoretical problems confronting sociolinguists, problems which are of crucial importance to language teachers.

What is a language?
Most of us would probably claim that we know what we mean when we say 'I speak English' or 'I speak French', but there are in fact a large number of difficulties associated with such statements. Even if we restrict the discussion to native speakers it is not entirely clear what such a statement tells us. We might think that it means 'I am intelligible to all other people who say they speak English', but there are many people who claim to be English-speaking who are not thus intelligible. Speakers of various urban and rural dialects of English are certainly not mutually intelligible, at least at first, while many people in the USA, the West Indies, India, South Africa and the South Pacific would also claim to be native speakers of English without being easily intelligible to each other. On the other hand, speakers of Norwegian and Danish can understand each other very often, and some people who speak German and live near the Dutch border speak a German dialect which linguists would describe as very close to the Dutch spoken on the other side of the border. We sometimes describe the language we speak in relation to political rather than linguistic boundaries. Yet at the same time the Americans and British would not wish to be thought of as one political unit on the basis of a common language, any more than the Mexicans and Spaniards would. Civil wars frequently show that a common language does not demonstrate interests held in common between two groups, so that clearly neither political nor economic nor geographical factors hold together speakers of a common language. It is true that some degree of historical contact is necessary between speakers of a particular language, but language changes over time and when it has to express different needs and belief systems, divergence is inevitable. There seem to be social factors determining what languages call themselves, and it is no doubt more prestigious to be associated with particular languages at particular times.

At the moment, English is dominant in the world as a whole. A number of factors account for this, including the imperial role—for better or worse—of Britain which has left many parts of the world with English as their main international language, and the economic and political dominance of the United States which has resulted in, for example, most scientific research being published in English and much political discussion, even between non-native-speaking countries, being conducted in English. This role has major political and economic implications for many countries. On the one hand intelligibility between all countries is desirable, but on the other linguistic imperialism can mean that only those speakers with access to English will be influential on the international scene or be able to exercise maximum control over their economies. Factors like this will affect what foreign languages are learnt, and also what languages people claim to speak, either as first or second languages. Speakers of a language which is fairly closely related to English may want to claim that it is English because that conveys potential social prestige, or they may want to insist (as some Americans do) on its independence from English because they wish to repudiate undesirable historical or moral associations.

In all such cases the decision will be only partly conscious and will be based on social and political criteria rather than formal linguistic ones. For these reasons, and because it is too difficult to find objective ways of measuring such aspects as mutual intelligibility, linguists tend to define a speech community as a group of people who claim to be speaking the same language or dialect, and to recognise that the claim is a social rather than a linguistic one.

Language and dialect

But the principles underlying our discussion of languages also underly discussion of any group of speakers, for no two people use identical dialects. The term 'dialect' is traditionally used to distinguish different varieties of the same language which reflect geographical distribution. There are, however, other causes of systematic variation between speakers. Different educational backgrounds, different social classes, different age groups, even different sexes may result in systematically different ways of speaking. In short, any difference between people which can be seen as socially significant can result in linguistic differences which are learnt and used as we acquire language. Some of these differences may relate only to communication between members of a particular group, but some may relate to communication with outsiders, and all societies have some forms of speech which are not reciprocal. We will say 'Your majesty' to a monarch, but we shall not expect to be addressed back as 'Your majesty'. On the other hand, members of a closed group may address each other as 'comrade' or 'brother' without necessarily extending such a privilege to outsiders. Forms of address are the most obvious examples of this dialectal feature, but it may show itself in syntax and selection of certain vocabulary items as well.

We find within a language, then, variations which enable us to recognise some characteristics of particular speakers. Some of these variations will be in pronunciation (usually referred to as 'accent'), some in syntax and some in vocabulary or in the meaning associated with commonly used words. We should remember, though, that any judgement about the existence of a dialect is a generalisation. We choose to pick out particular characteristics and to see linguistic characteristics associated with non-linguistic ones. Such an identi- fication between linguistic and non-linguistic factors may be accep- ted by speakers of a dialect, or it may not. Parents frequently try to bring their children up without some features of the local dialect and not everyone likes to have his 'English' identified by outsiders as marked for a particular region or educational background. The judgements, as with judgements about particular languages, are social and reflect social prejudices and stereotypings which may or may not be sympathetic. Nor should such issues be seen as trivial. Many lives have been lost over political arguments at least partly centred on language issues, and in Britain passions can be roused over discussions of desirable and undesirable forms of speech. As teachers, we shall of course have to consider the educational implications of such factors, which will be discussed in Chapter Nine, but as sociolinguists we have a duty to note (as accurately as possible) how people behave in order that our judgements may be based on a realistic assessment of the situation.

Register

In the previous section we have considered how language may vary from speaker to speaker. Even a statement such as this oversim- plifies, in fact, for people do choose to some extent whether to operate a particular dialect or not. Many students feel that their dialect changes slightly when they move from college to home, or from one part of the country to another, and any speaker who never changed dialectal forms would sound odd to at least some of the people he spoke to. Quite apart from this aspect, however, we regularly change our style in relation to our speech situation. We will not speak in the same way in a law court, a school classroom, a pub and a church. Nor will our language remain exactly the same if we switch topic within the same situation. Language related to sport will differ syntactically from language related to political discussion or scientific description. Furthermore, the language appropriate to casual conversation will be different from that used in a formal lecture, that used to a person much older will differ from that used to a person much younger, and so on.

Discussion of such issues as this has been called the study of 'register' and, although the meaning of the term is hard to define exactly, it is retained here for convenience and because so many people still use it. Early studies of different registers, or 'functional dialects', tended to concentrate on the vocabulary being used, which clearly differs markedly from topic to topic. However, it soon became apparent that syntax and phonology changed also according to *what* was being said to *whom*, *where* and through *what means*. And as studies progressed linguists found that discourse features became of greater and greater interest. Sometimes it proved helpful to consider rhetorical devices through which the speech or writing was organised into a shape appropriate for its purpose. In speech, analysis of procedures for interaction between speakers became important, while in writing language had to be considered in relation to factors like design and the use of non-linguistic signalling systems such as diagrams and pictures. As soon as it became apparent that language operated as a system in relation to other systems, discussion of language in isolation became both harder and less useful, for messages are rarely conveyed solely by language: a fuller context needs to be taken into account. But we are only just beginning to be able to describe the main elements of that context, and it will be some time before it will be easy to explain the full structure of human communication.

It is not only problems with the relationship to context which make 'register' difficult to define. There is an even more fundamental difficulty. Each time we describe a new register we have to define its features in relation to other registers. Most discussion assumes that there is some sort of 'common core' of language and that there are certain distinctive forms which deviate from the common core. But of course the common core consists of language being used for specfic purposes—there is no language independent of its use. We thus frequently find ourselves with a circular argument in which we recognise—say—the language of law by its peculiar features, and then carefully define its peculiar features, saying that we have thereby defined it. All we have done is to reinforce our own stereotypes. Now this may have some value when we are looking at a style like legal style which is recognised as distinctive by everyone, but it makes it very hard for us to define with any subtlety and usefulness when we are talking about less specialised uses of language. Any use of language is rich in potential variation and too narrow an analysis of appropriate styles invariably becomes simplistic. This is particularly important in teaching, because we cannot afford to be too rigid about the degree of stylistic variation that we accept for particular purposes from our students; yet of course there *are* limits to what is acceptable. Unfortunately it is really easier to define what is inappropriate than what is appropriate, which poses a major problem for teachers who do not want to appear too negative to their students.

Static and dynamic models

Sociolinguistics has moved linguistics into a direct confrontation with a problem central to all discussions of language teaching. Traditional formal linguistics has had to generalise and idealise. People do not talk as consistently and unvariably as grammar books imply they ought to. Above all, they do not talk in order to produce isolated sentences. They speak for a whole variety of purposes, usually (though not always) to communicate something to other people. They speak in messages, not in grammatical categories, and they do not possess their language, they use it, they do things with it. And when we learn language, whether we are acquiring a new one or increasing our ability to use our mother tongue (that is, developing the use of a wider range of dialects and registers in it), we are learning to do something, not to possess something. This is an important point, for if we possess something it does not change, but we cannot learn language without changing it for our own purposes. Insofar as we have purposes for ourselves different from those of other people, our use of language will be slightly different from theirs. Language change is no more than the collective different ways in which

47

individuals find it convenient to change their personal use of the language. Individuals do not usually change in isolation because it takes two to create an understood message and many to establish a convention, but the language cannot but change as long as we each have anything new to say. Thus language use and language change are one and the same thing. Furthermore language *learning* and language *use* are the same thing. In the native speaker situation children learn to use their language and learn the formal features that it possesses in ways which are impossible to disentangle. The biggest problem in most foreign language learning situations is that use and learning have become separated. But both language learning, however artificial, and language use are dynamic: the language changes from speaker to speaker, situation, setting, and it also changes as each speaker matures. Imagine the complexity of the currents and winds on the sea, or a great lake, and then imagine an analysis based on a still photograph. Such an analysis is what the formal linguist is engaged in.

To say all this is not to attack formal linguistics. Such a limitation is essential, for we cannot understand something as complex as language without simplifying and regularising. But language teachers are working with real people and must return to the dynamic model. They want their students to be able to operate a system which can be described by the linguist's static model, but they are not teaching that model, they are teaching how to *use* language, not how to make a static description. Luckily, it is not as difficult to teach the former as the latter.

In order to understand more fully the process of language change, we shall have to look more closely at the whole process of variation—and that is likely to be one of the major concerns of the next twenty years. Meanwhile, the language teacher can concentrate on the process of language learning, making sure that the methodology adopted allows students to use language dynamically rather than learn and possess it passively. It is highly probable that sociolinguistic insights will contribute a great deal to our understanding of the process of learning to use language, but it is too early to be certain.

Languages, pidgins and creoles

Not only does the language of an individual change, but languages themselves blend, dissolve, separate, and even die. The process is slow, of course, but it is easy to see how such apparently catastrophic events must occur, for all human groupings must evolve a means of communication and as economic and political pressures change relations between people, so languages will adapt to reflect these changes. If, for example, French and English speakers had a great deal of contact over a long period in comparative isolation from the rest of the world and with strong pressures to combine as one community, a combined language would inevitably emerge. No doubt the process of combining would be painful, with groups for the defence of each language being active, but the only way to avoid the emergence of a combined language would be for social pressures to force the two communities apart again. It is worth noting that one of the social pressures which might do that could be the desire to retain a 'pure' language, if such a desire were promoted sufficiently strongly; the situation is not one of being at the mercy of uncontrollable pressures. Nonetheless, economic forces are difficult to fight against, and linguistic pressure groups reflect a variety of non-linguistic motivations as well as linguistic ones.

Logic, as well as experience, suggests that there may be three stages in the development of a new language. In the first stage a means of communication will develop between two groups who need contact. It will be nobody's first language, but it will be a useful communication tool for certain restricted purposes, and its grammar, and its vocabulary, will reflect its limited use. This will be technically a 'pidgin'. As more and more people become assimilated into the intermediate culture, gradually the language will be required for more and more aspects of life until native speakers appear, and the language has become a 'creole'. It will still be recognisably the descendant of the two original languages, and there will probably be considerable snobbish belittling of the 'hybrid' at least as long as the two older languages survive in relatively pure form or until contact is lost with the two original cultures. Only then will the language be accorded full status as a language. This description is oversimplified, but it reflects the gradual transition of most languages from the status of pidgins, to creoles, and finally to 'languages'. Note that there is a clear difference in function between the first two, but that the difference between the last two depends more on the attitude people take to them. A creole may have a literature and all the characteristics of any other language. It is unfortunate that terms which are widely interpreted as derogatory are used also in this technical sense, for they have overtones of colonialism which

49

interfere with many people's response to them. English is technically a creole by this definition, except that with creoles you can usually see another language in relation to which their development can be measured. In fact, the process of linguistic change will always involve some degree of creolisation.

Many people now consider that linguistics is being forced to become the study of language variation: core linguistics is seen as simply the preliminary to the systematic study of linguistic variability. Whether or not we wish to accept such a strong claim, we can certainly concede that no language teacher can afford to remain ignorant of such studies, for language teachers have a strong vested interest in language change.

6 How we study style: stylistics

To most people it appears obvious that any discipline which has something useful to say about language must also have something useful to say about literature. Certainly, linguists and literary critics have for a long time considered literature from a linguistic point of view. However, there is by no means agreement about the best ways for linguistic understanding to be related to literary understanding, nor about the status of literary texts in relation to linguistic studies. Indeed, it may well be argued that there can be no specifically *linguistic* study of literary texts which will throw light on their literary qualities.

The situation has been further complicated by linguists and literary critics becoming unnecessarily suspicious of each other, each accusing the other of trespassing on their territory without appropriate intellectual equipment. Such an argument is rather pointless, and can be simply resolved, but that has not prevented discussion from being fierce and misunderstanding frequent. We should be able to accept, though, that if explicit statements are to be made about language (whether literary texts or any other form of language), then such statements should be backed by evidence using the procedures of linguistics, for linguistics is the only discipline which has been developed for that specific purpose. However, if we are to concern ourselves with the *significance* of such statements, then the traditions and procedures of literary criticism may be more appropriate. (It should not be forgotten, of course, that one person may simultaneously possess skills, and training, in both literary criticism and linguistics.) Thus, if we want to claim, for example, that certain features of D. H. Lawrence's style are reminiscent of the Authorised

51

Version of the Bible, we may be able to do this satisfactorily enough for our argument by simply placing two appropriate extracts together. If we want to make a wider claim of this kind, however, we shall have to use terminology and tools of description which have been tried on other similar exercises of comparison—in other words the tools of descriptive linguistics. But having decided, and proved, that there are these similarities in style, we have not yet made a statement of particular interest about Lawrence's work—there are no doubt many forgotten novelists whose style is similarly reminiscent of the Authorised Version. To assess the significance of this observation in relation to the twentieth century novel, or Lawrence's development as a writer, or the message which Lawrence intends to convey, is a task for which the linguist, as linguist, has no particular competence, but which literary critics are particularly trained to work on. Linguistics is a tool for the critic, and if he ignores it, he runs the risk of making unsupported assertions, but a descriptive science cannot do more than quantify.

For the linguist, there are a number of other problems to be clarified in discussing literature. Literature has been referred to sometimes as a language variety, but in what ways can it be considered one particular variety? Is there one particular style distinctive of literary works? It is rather difficult to see how there can be, for writers are free to exploit all the resources of the language. Yet there are recognisable styles associated with particular writers, with particular periods and with particular types of writing. What has linguistics to offer in the classification of these stylistic features?

It might appear easy simply to list all the interesting features of the language of a particular poet, or period, and to describe them in linguistic terms, but in fact doing this precisely is a very difficult task. This is because, if we want to isolate the characteristic features of a particular corpus of language, we have to compare it with other language in order to see how it differs. Now, what other language should we compare a poet's work with? Presumably the work of other poets. What language should the literature of a particular period be compared with? Presumably with the literature of some other period. Leaving aside a number of tricky problems of definition (when does a period start and stop? which of a writer's works count as literature and which do not?), it will be clear that any serious comparison of a large body of language with another large body will be a very time-consuming task. In practice, both linguists and critics pick out features of language which conveniently support their arguments, but they are unable to produce an objective description of the 'style' of a body of literature as a whole. Furthermore, while we may have intuitions about a certain kind of writing deviating from a 'norm' of ordinary language, we must bear in mind that that 'norm' consists of language fulfilling ordinary purposes, that is being adapted to particular uses, each of which make their own stylistic demands on the language being used. Language which had no characteristic style would be meaningless, because the style results from the choices we make to achieve communication. In fact it becomes increasingly apparent as we attempt to describe literary texts that we can only do so by becoming more aware of *all* uses of language. The writer exploits historical and contemporary sources of language use, oral and written, to achieve the desired effects and if the linguist wishes to describe precisely what is happening, he will have to have available precise descriptions of non-literary language for comparison.

Stylistics, then, must be seen as a part of the study of language varieties, and such studies are still in their infancy. Nonetheless, in recent years there has been a large number of literary critics whose work has both influenced and been influenced by linguistics, and some of their approaches to literature are described below.

Structuralism
Studies of language have been most successful when examining its formal properties. Particularly at the levels of sound and grammar, as we have seen, language can be seen as a structured system in which the parts are considered in terms of their relationship with each other. Such an approach to the study of language goes back to the work of the Swiss linguist, Saussure, at the beginning of this century. As we indicated earlier in this chapter, literary studies can be considered simply as descriptive work within the straightforward linguistic tradition. However, a number of scholars in disciplines outside linguistics have attempted to consider their own disciplines from the same sort of 'structuralist' point of view as Saussure used for language. Some of these attempts have fed back into literary studies through literary critics with a particular interest in plot, myth and language.

In western Europe the major influence in this direction has been the French anthropologist, Claude Lévi-Strauss. He has set out to apply to the study of social life the procedures of twentieth century linguistics —and, indeed, he has suggested that phenomena such as art and religion may have the same kind of structure as human language. The implication is that language reflects in its organisation the structure of all human symbolic systems, whatever the particular nature of the symbols through which such systems are expressed. Similarly, just as each language is internally coherent, and is best defined in its own terms, so the understanding of another culture will be made possible by investigating the relationships between its significant myths and the categories of thought which these establish and reinforce. Such an analysis of significant myths had direct implications for the study of literature, for literature too is a creating of significance by use of descriptions of events in a fictional world. If the structuring of human language and the structuring of human stories are in some sense systematically parallel, then we should be helped to see more clearly the relationships between the language and the meanings of literary texts, especially if the meanings can be connected with the beliefs of a particular society about the nature of reality.

Studies of this kind may suggest exciting possibilities for literary criticism, but it is another tradition which has looked most closely at conventional literary texts. A number of Russian critics in the 1920s were developing a school of criticism which anticipated the link with the linguists of the structural anthropologists many years later. Indeed, one of their number, Roman Jakobson, was a major contributor to both literary and formal linguistic studies, both in the Soviet Union and—later—in the United States. The Russian formalists were particularly concerned with literary structure, in an attempt to define what it was that made a work of literature 'literary'. Particularly, they were concerned to isolate the devices by which writers 'made strange' the world in which we live, that is how writers use language to make us see what they refer to in a new light. A soft version of this argument would simply see the writer as enabling his readers to view the world differently, but a hard version—to which later formalist writing was led—would see the process of making strange as self-justifying. That is, the artist's preoccupation with artistic form means that it is the process of creating a work of art which is what all art is 'about'. Both implications have been developed by later writers. Brecht's 'alienation', for example, is an illustration of the weak argument, for, by emphasising the distance between the play and the audience, he forces the audience to evaluate the images, and not to enter the story and merely respond uncritically. The strong argument leads ultimately to an emphasis on the artistic process for its own sake which has been significant for both writers and critics, as we shall see below. The procedures of the formalists, then, link with both Saussurean linguistics and with the work of Lévi-Strauss in their concern for the structure of stories analysed through the relationships between events, the ways in which typical characters operate, and so on. Literature is seen as a system with its own conventions, which can be defined by the ways in which the parts interact. The risk, however, with this approach, is that literature becomes divorced from anything else. The writers are, after all, using language which we all use, and operating with symbols and cultural values which we must share if we are to be able to understand them at all. What is clear, though, is that literature employs a complex network of relationships which writers and readers manipulate and respond to both consciously and unconsciously. Some critics, most notably Jakobson, would see literature in the context of general language use, and certainly the systems which writers operate include the general functions of language which all of us use in our everyday lives, referred to in Chapter Five.

The strong argument referred to in the previous paragraph appears very interestingly in the critical work of the Frenchman, Roland Barthes. He insists that works of literature are frequently self-justifying, they convey no external message but are about the process of writing itself. Such an assertion only makes sense in the context of an analysis of the act of reading: in many everyday situations we do indeed use language referring to external objects and events, but when we read a work of literature we may be responding to, and becoming aware of, a complex network of cultural signals—for literature is distinguished by the self-consciousness of its cultural reference. Thus literature is not important for *what* it says but for the way in which it makes us aware of conventions by its manipulating of them. The style *is* the message. The process of reading becomes an active engagement with the text, in which the reader creates meaning for himself out of the conflicts and ambiguities of the text.

Barthes associates his stylistic studies with a complex system of analysis of signs and conventions. In part, he is arguing most strongly against the particularly French tradition of limpid clarity in literary texts in which—it is implied—there is one clear and unambiguous reading possible. But it is clear that his ideas, like those of a number of sociologists, anthropologists and linguists such as Whorf, Bernstein and Lévi-Strauss, are concerned with the relationship between language, myth, thought and ideology. Such concerns are vitally important for education as well as for literature, but they take us outside the realm of linguistics proper, if only because the questions being asked are so vast in their implications and at the moment so incapable of rigorous solution that an empirical science has little to contribute. However, it is important to recognise the connections with linguistics of such work in peripheral areas, for it may eventually provide a connection between formal linguistic studies and work on the uses to which we put our knowledge of language.

Stylistics can be seen, then, as a branch of descriptive linguistics, or it can be linked with broader anthropological and literary studies as part of a total science of signs. The danger of the former approach is that it may degenerate into mere data collection (syllable counting, undirected analysis of syntactic patterns, for example); the danger of the latter approach is that it becomes such a vast subject that it can only be talked about vaguely and speculatively. But because literature is of such absorbing interest to many scholars, the role of linguistics in literary study will continue to preoccupy linguists, however uncertain the precise status of stylistics. For the teacher of language or literature, the best guidance to offer is probably to recommend as thorough an understanding of the organisation of English as possible, to be applied to literary texts only when such understanding seems genuinely to illuminate a sensitive reading of the text.

Thus any literary critic who points out the significance of sentence structure in a poem, or of the relationships between sound patterning and meaning—that is, any critic who tries to relate the meaning of the text to the linguistic structure—is engaged in stylistics. But everything that can be said about a text is not necessarily significant. To the theoretical linguist, a literary text is one among many examples of language in use. To the literary critic, linguistics is one of a number of useful sciences from which tools for analysis can be taken. Insofar as stylistics is a descriptive science, it is part of linguistics; insofar as it aids evaluation, it is a tool of literary criticism. In practice, people claim to be 'doing stylistics' for a wide range of different purposes, and insights deriving from work in stylistics may appear—indirectly—in any discussion of language varieties. But more than most of the linguistic sciences it suffers from having potentially unlimited ambitions, and too many people, with too many differing aims, claiming allegiance to it. Most discussions of the relevance of stylistics to teaching either language or literature are simply discussions of the relevance of the procedures of descriptive linguistics to these activities.

7 What happens inside: psycholinguistics

Psycholinguistics is the branch of study concerned with the investigation of the mental processes underlying the learning and using of language. As its name suggests, it combines knowledge drawn from psychology with knowledge drawn from linguistics. Chapter Eleven, which deals with psychology and language teaching, discusses some of the implications of psycholinguistic research, as well as of general psychology, for teaching practice, but the present chapter concentrates more on psycholinguistic theory and less on how this might influence what the teacher does. It also leaves out of account certain more general psychological factors which may have a bearing on language learning in the individual case. However, we must make it clear that there is no hard and fast division to be drawn between psychology and psycholinguistics, or between, say, psycholinguistics and the psychology of language learning; they are part of the same continuum, and which one one claims to be doing will be determined by one's particular focus of interest at the time. Our division in this book is largely a matter of convenience.

An important branch of psycholinguistics is *developmental psycholinguistics*, which is concerned with the development of language in children, and with the relationship between the development of language and the development of other faculties and abilities. The sorts of questions which developmental psycholinguists are interested in are: How do children learn language? How long does it take them? In what sequence do they learn the various parts of the system representing a language? Can they think or reason in any significant sense before they have learnt language, or does *cognitive development* (the development of reasoning) depend upon the development of language? If so, to what extent? How do children acquire meaning? To what extent do parents and children's companions influence their linguistic development? Is there any sense in which they are taught their mother tongue? More generally, psycholinguists are concerned with problems such as how we *encode* speech (plan it and put it together) and *decode* it (extract the meaning from it); whether speech is guided by a system of rules or a system of habits; what the relationship is between language and memory; whether, when we encode complex sentences, we start out from simpler structures, and so on. Many of the questions to which psycholinguists would like an answer in fact lead into the study of *neurolinguistics*, which seeks to investigate the relationship between language and the structure and functioning of the brain and the nervous system.

In a dual-pronged study like psycholinguistics, each 'side' will naturally look to see whether its findings seem to be confirmed by those of the other 'side', and each will seek information from the other. This is potentially stimulating, but it can have the disadvantage that if the one 'side' has the wrong picture of things, it will hold back the other 'side'. If the linguists say, 'Language is like this, not like that', the psychologists will have to take them seriously, whether they are right or wrong, and if the psychologists say. 'The mind works like this, not like that', the linguists will again probably tend to maintain consistency with the psychologists, whether they are right or wrong. Actually, we do not know who is ultimately right and who is wrong in these matters; we are not at a stage at which there are many established facts, but rather, differing degrees of plausibil- ity between different ideas. However, if a study like psycholinguistics has brought any advantage, it is precisely that both linguists and psychologists concerned with language are co-operating more closely than ever before, and there is a concern among linguists to try to establish that the descriptions they produce possess *psychological reality*, that is, give a picture of language which is consistent with what we know of the workings of the human mind. The model of language which has made the greatest claim to possessing 'psychological reality' is transformational generative grammar, and though this claim has proved extremely controversial, psycholinguists have found at least some evidence that it conforms with what we know of the mechanisms underlying speech. There is, however, a possible circularity in this, because they have been prompted by this particular model of language to look for those mechanisms with which it would be consistent; and if they were working with some other model of language, they might look for, and find, evidence of other mechanisms suggested by it of which we at present have little or no inkling.

Transformational generative grammar is in fact, in general terms, the 'accepted' basis for most current work in psycholinguistics, but rather than go into much detail about this current work, we propose to limit ourselves to contrasting the two major sources of psycholinguistic ideas in this century: the ideas stemming from behaviourist psychology and structuralist linguistics on the one hand, and those stemming from Chomskyan linguistics on the other. It is true that for most specialists behaviourist psycholinguistics is now 'old hat'; however, few directions in thought have ever had such a profound influence upon educational theory and practice, or upon language learning and teaching, as behaviourism, whose influence is still quite evident today, however research may have changed direction in more recent years. Chomskyan linguistics represented a fierce challenge to behaviourism, and in its own way has also exerted a profound influence on education, particularly with regard to language teaching. We shall add to our account a brief discussion of the concept of language learning as against language acquisition.

Empiricism and 'verbal behaviour'

It is to behaviourist psychology on the one hand and to structuralist linguistics on the other that the origins of psycholinguistics are to be credited. Even though the term 'psycholinguistics' has only recently become common currency, almost everything else which has taken place in psycholinguistic research has stemmed from a reaction to these beginnings in the early part of this century. Behaviourist psychology and structuralist linguistics were in fact remarkably well twinned from the outset to the extent that both were, ultimately as a matter of dogma, interested only in founding knowledge upon what could be directly observed, and the philosophy on which they were based is often referred to as 'empiricism'. In the end, the tension between adopting methods of investigation requiring concentration on observable behaviour, on the one hand, and the desire to investigate matters in which so much is not directly observable, on the other, proved too great; but at least the foundations for a new type of study had been laid.

The initial impetus for behaviourist psychology, and also, indirectly, for the first steps in psycholinguistic research, derived from the Russian scientist Pavlov and his *conditioning* experiments. For him, all behaviour could potentially be accounted for in terms of *stimuli*, that is, things which arouse or excite reactions, and *responses*, that is, the reactions or behaviours aroused by the stimuli. Pavlov had observed that if he gave an animal—typically, a dog—some bread to eat, the animal would salivate on having the food placed in its mouth. (Pavlov actually measured salivation at source, by tapping digestive juices through a tube from the glands producing them.) Salivation, then, was a response to the stimulus provided by the food, and, in the circumstances described, Pavlov designated this response as an *unconditional reflex*, that is, a 'natural', inborn response which has not had to be learnt. But Pavlov discovered that the same response could be 'schooled', or *conditioned*, since, once his experimental animals became used to receiving food from him, the mere sight of food being brought would be sufficient to excite salivation in them. Pavlov assumed that this time the response was not inborn, but was a *conditional reflex*, learnt by *association*. But he also showed that stimuli, as well as responses, can be conditional. If, over a period of time, a bell was rung whenever a dog was presented with food, and then the bell was rung without any food being presented, the animal would still respond to the bell by salivating, because it now *associated* the ringing of the bell with food. So a response which had not existed 'naturally' was now being produced by a stimulus which had not existed 'naturally'.

Pavlov believed that the process of association, whereby new connections are made between stimuli and responses, was to be explained in physiological terms, as the result of the creation of new pathways within the nervous system. In a way, his experiments with salivation may appear relatively trivial, but what he discovered can be perceived as anything but trivial if one considers that the whole process of learning could now be viewed as one in which, through association, a relatively small set of unconditional reflexes could gradually develop into a more complex system of conditional reflexes, and a set of prime stimuli could branch out into a more complex set of conditional stimuli, culminating in a vast network of stimuli and responses which accounted for the behaviour of a living organism.

Another concept emerging from the work of Pavlov and the behaviourist psychologists is that of *reinforcement*. Pavlov himself had found in his experiments with conditional reflexes that if he tried to excite a conditional reflex in an animal by showing it food or ringing a bell, but constantly withheld the food itself, the conditional reflex, though occurring at first, would eventually become *extinguished*: association would have broken down. What psychologists concluded from this sort of evidence was that if a certain behaviour, a certain response, is to be maintained, then every so often it must be strengthened, or *reinforced*, by appropriate satisfaction, be this food or whatever else might be desired. Applied to human psychology, an idea which people had long subscribed to intuitively now seemed to have 'scientific' status; give rewards for behaviour which is to be encouraged, and this behaviour will become entrenched; withhold rewards, and it is likely to weaken and eventually disappear. By the same token, if there are behaviours which need positive discouragement, then under no circumstances must they ever be reinforced by any sort of reward. Indeed, some behaviourist psychologists gave 'scientific' status to the idea of *negative reinforcement*, or punishment, for undesirable behaviour: punish a 'bad' response, and it will disappear all the more quickly. Again, of course, this seems like a piece of common sense to many people, and it is implicit in the legal codes and practices of most, if not all, societies. The extent to which things actually work like this, however, still remains open to question, especially where human beings are concerned, and the behaviourists, despite their success in experiments with animals under laboratory conditions, did not in the end manage to demonstrate 'scientifically' the centrality of reward and punishment to all behaviour. Nevertheless, the concepts of reinforcement and negative reinforcement are still being 'applied' in fields such as 'behaviour therapy', and are not without influence among educators.

Though we may now seem to have moved a long way from the question of language, we have in fact come very near to the crux of the behaviourists' view of it. We can say this because, whether they could in the end prove it or not, many behaviourists working with the stimulus-response model soon became convinced that it could potentially account for *all* learning and behaviour, and the structuralist linguists of the time did little to discourage them in their belief that language was simply a behavioural system: *verbal behaviour*. In other words, language was the manifestation of a network of habits built up through conditioning and association in much the same way as any other sort of behaviour; and in essence this is the conception put forward by the American psychologist Skinner in his well known book, *Verbal Behaviour*.

It is true that Skinner and other behaviourists extended and modified Pavlov's original ideas, with Skinner himself introducing the notion of *operant conditioning*, a key concept in his own account of verbal behaviour. This type of conditioning differs from the classical conditioning demonstrated by Pavlov in that it does not assume that an experimenter or any other agency in the environment needs to provide a particular initial stimulus in order to produce a response which can subsequently be conditioned through reinforcement. What happens, at least in the laboratory, is that an experimental animal does something seemingly of its own accord (though what it does would technically be regarded as a response to some stimulus or other, whose nature, however, need not be of any interest where this procedure is being employed) and that the experimenter then sets out to reinforce this behaviour, or response. For example, if a pigeon happens to lift up a wing, the experimenter might immediately give it some food, and do likewise on every subsequent occasion on which it does so, until the pigeon has associated lifting its wing with being given food. Now the situation has changed, as the pigeon will lift its wing *in order* to obtain food, so that, provided the experimenter keeps up the reinforcement with sufficient frequency, the lifting of the wing will have become and will remain a conditional reflex. Again, the particular example given may seem trivial, but once the principle is generalised, it may be seen as a most attractive idea in the explanation of learning and behaviour. Applied to verbal behaviour, for instance, it relieves one of the burden of trying to match up every sound or utterance a person produces with a known initial stimulus, a task which is in any case impossible because everyone, from youngest child to adult, so often produces sounds and utterances with seeming spontaneity, without the stimulus for so doing being in the least obvious or observable. But what one can say from this point, insofar as one accepts Skinner's idea as at all plausible, is that the reception that such sounds or utterances meet with will either reinforce or not reinforce the verbal behaviour in question, so that a person's total verbal behaviour will be a system of habitual responses cultivated, or 'shaped', through reinforcement. Parental approval of a sound such as 'dad dad', for example, will in theory strengthen the likelihood of its re-occurrence, and even though it may start off as some 'natural', unconditional reflex, reinforcement will eventually condition it, and the process of association will render it a habitual response within a certain context (in this case, no doubt, presence of father). However, while it is possible to see that the notion of operant conditioning provides some sort of basis on which to build up a view of the mechanics of language learning, as a process in which unconditional reflexes become conditioned, sounds become associated through reinforcement with other sounds, words become associated through reinforcement with other words, and so on, on its own it provides no answer to many points of technical detail which must be addressed in any learning theory. How do we account, for example, for the person whose verbal behaviour is inappropriate, perhaps by being invariably tactless and giving offence? Since this type of behaviour is unlikely to be reinforced by the people on the receiving end of it, we would have to begin to assume reinforcement by factors so complex and processes so tortuous that in the end the theory becomes inelegant and unwieldy.

Although in popularised versions of behaviourist learning theory, especially as applied to verbal behaviour, it is usually Skinner who receives the greatest attention, his was in fact only one theory among several which sought to extend the basic stimulus-response model into a powerful explanation of learning and behaviour. As none of these theories would now appear tenable, at least as total explanations, we will not go further into the details. However, we should note two concepts associated with the work of the behaviourists generally which have had a significant impact on thought about language learning and language teaching. The first of these is *drive*, or, as it is known more popularly, *motivation*, which is the impelling force felt or demonstrated by an individual in carrying out a task. It has been suggested that motivation may be positive or negative, or both at the same time. Negative motivation, not to be confused with lack of motivation, amounts to fear of the consequences of *not* doing what one is supposed to do; fear, for example, of the disapproval, or worse, of parents or teachers. Positive motivation, on the other hand, stems from the desire or need to gain rewards or satisfaction. The behaviourists saw motivation, however, less as a mental state than as a physiological urge which craves relief and which consequently drives the organism it affects to seek this relief in the most appropriate way. Behaviouristic thought about first language learning, then, suggested that children were strongly motivated to learn the mother tongue because language could be used as an instrument for making needs known efficiently and having them satisfied. It was assumed that all children would be equally motivated in this respect when they had no language at all to use in the fulfilment of their needs, but when it came to second or foreign language learning it was assumed that the circumstances of individuals would vary greatly, with some being motivated more than others, and that different degrees of motivation would largely explain different degrees of success. The second concept, or, more precisely, set of concepts, we should note here, is that of *imitation* and *practice*. The idea of learning through imitation is actually a very ancient one, and long before the advent of behaviourism educationists had observed that children seemed to be endowed with enormous imitative capacities which enabled them to learn many skills very quickly. The behaviourists looked upon imitation more formally, however, as a necessary process in the learning of new responses, and held that further practice, subsequent to initial imitation, strengthened a response and ensured its entry into an individual's set of habitual behaviours. It seemed 'obvious' enough that imitation and practice were natural and, indeed, essential, to first language learning, and though, again, these devices had been extensively employed in second language teaching long before behaviourist psychology came into being, their adoption as formal concepts in behaviourist psychology seemed to lend them additional justification as second language teaching techniques.

We have said that structuralist linguistics did nothing to discourage the behaviourist view that language was simply a behavioural system. Much of the reason for this is that the structuralists made no greatly principled distinction between *language* as a system of rules and *speech* as the manifestation of language through utterances. Though they may well have accepted that the production of speech was controlled by a set of 'blueprints' ingrained in the nervous system, they did not consider that the structure underlying an utterance and the structure of the utterance itself could be quite different in many respects, or, to put it in the terms used in Chapter Two, that there may be profound differences between *deep structure* and *surface structure*. Thus sentences like 'John is easy to please' and 'John is eager to please' would both have appeared to proceed from the same 'blueprint': noun + copula (is) + adjective + infinitive. As we shall see, there are reasons for thinking—in the light of transformational generative grammar—that the structures underlying the two sentences quoted are entirely different, as are the relationships between the elements in them. However, it can be seen that, while structuralism held sway, learning a language could be viewed largely as the learning of a set of sentence patterns and of items of vocabulary to be slotted into them in a fairly mechanical way. Moreover, the picture of language presented by the structuralists suggested that it is arranged in some sense in a straightforward serial order. This suited behaviourist psychology because the theory of association, as the mechanism enabling new responses to be learnt and old ones to be expanded, could only remain plausible as long as learning and behaviour could be regarded as having a serial order to them. And if sentences could be considered to possess a serially-ordered structure, it was possible to see them as 'associative chains' even to the extent of hypothesising that each word in an utterance was selected by association with the previous word in a 'left-to-right' process. So the constructing of a sentence might be seen as a procedure not unlike that of playing dominoes—the second piece cannot be selected or laid before the first piece has been placed, and so on.

The first doubts about the structuralist-behaviourist conception of language actually came from certain behaviourists themselves who were not satisfied with the idea of 'associative chains', since evidence gathered, for example, from observation of slips of the tongue, in which people might reverse the normal order of words in utterances, suggested that the selection of words did not take place by simple association and that the system underlying language was not 'linear'. The problem was, however, that the structuralists and the behaviourists had no framework for dealing with the complexities involved, or even for seeing them adequately, and it is to the American linguist Chomsky that the credit must go for shedding new light on the processes underlying the learning and using of language, and also, ultimately, for inspiring psycholinguistics as it is conceived today. Nevertheless, behaviourist ideas about language and language learning have had such an impact on language teaching in this century that they cannot simply be ignored.

Mentalism and language as an innate faculty

The view of language represented by Chomsky is often referred to as 'mentalist' because it sees language not as conditioned, stimulus-bound verbal behaviour but as a property of the mind. This mentalist view evolved, in the course of Chomsky's work, from what was initially a preoccupation with the technicalities of language. We cannot go fully into these technicalities here, but to give an example of the sort of problems which interested Chomsky, we might return to the two sentences already quoted: 'John is easy to please' and 'John is eager to please'. As stated, the structuralists would have regarded these sentences as possessing the same structure, or as being different realisations of the same sentence pattern. To look at them in these terms, however, is to miss the important observation that native speakers of English are immediately aware that the sentences express different relationships between the elements within them, the first implying that someone other than John is doing the pleasing when John is pleased, and the second that John will be doing the pleasing when the chance to please arises. The two sentences may well share the same surface structure, then, but their underlying, or deep, structures are different, being respectively something like: 'It is easy for someone/someone please John' and 'John eager/John please someone'. Looking only at the surface structure of the two sentences, one would say that in both cases John is the subject; but now, looking at the deep structures, one can see that in the one case 'John' must be regarded as the object, and in the other case as the subject. The fact that native speakers perceive this sort of distinction intuitively (even if they cannot express it in grammatical terminology) indicates that they have a knowledge of language which is highly abstract. Furthermore, the fact that native speakers would also recognise that 'It is easy to please John' is a perfectly grammatical variant of 'John is easy to please', whereas 'It is eager to please John' (where the 'it' is impersonal) is not a grammatical variant of 'John is easy to please', indicates that they are aware of the *rules* of their language; rules far more complex and intricate than these examples can bring out.

For Chomsky, further evidence that language is to be regarded as *rule governed* rather than as a system of conditioned responses is that human beings use it *innovatively* and *creatively*. While there might be certain set patterns of speech which are predictable in certain situations—the forms of greetings and apologies, for example—the way sentences are constructed and combined, and the words used in them, are in most situations quite unpredictable in any precise sense. Anyone sceptical of this claim might like to try writing down the sentences on the next page of this book before reading the page. At least two things follow from the fact that we can construct and understand sentences which are entirely 'novel'. One is that if they are novel, we cannot have learnt them through some simple process of imitation and practice, neither can they be part of a repertoire of conditioned responses. The other is that since we cannot have learnt novel sentences as such in advance, the best explanation available to us at present of our ability to construct and understand them would seem to be that we have acquired, and share, knowledge of the principles governing the construction of sentences, and of the principles through which sound is related to meaning. We might add to this that given the vast, indeed infinite, possibilities for sentence construction and combination, even one lifetime would not be enough to learn all possible sentences, if the learning of a language depended on the building up of a network of linguistic 'habits'. So, to put the implications of Chomsky's work in the correct perspective, these are that native speakers of a language, by virtue of knowing the rules of their language, can *potentially* produce and understand all the possible sentences of the language as well as recognise any non-sentence, that is, ungrammatical sequence, produced in the language.

We noted in Chapter Two that speech is in fact divided up into utterances, not words and sentences, but that, in order to be able to investigate the regularities underlying speech, linguists are obliged to 'idealise' if they wish to investigate *language* as this system of regularities rather than *speech*. In speech, this system of regularities is certainly available to both speakers and hearers, but is often 'obscured' in the sense that, when speaking, people are capable of doing all sorts of unsystematic things such as pausing, changing their minds in mid-flow about what they want to say, losing the thread of their arguments, getting muddled up, and being in general 'ungrammatical'. In order to clear the way for his own investigations as a linguist, then, Chomsky put forward the distinction between *competence*, as our knowledge of language as a system of regularities, and *performance*, as actual instances of use of language in speech, proposing to limit his investigations to the former. But, to study competence, he also needed to propose a further 'idealisation': to ignore the individual differences between people with regard to language and to assume that the same generalities applied universally. This idealisation has proved controversial among those concerned with individuals in real life language learning and language using situations, and in relation to language teaching in particular the idea of linguistic competence has been superseded by that of *communicative competence* (see Chapter Eight), though this concept itself would undoubtedly not have developed if Chomsky had not put forward the notion of linguistic competence in the first place. But in any case it is important not to misunderstand the purpose of Chomsky's approach to the study of language: this is not focused on the details of the individual, but concerned with a faculty, or mental property, with which all human beings are in principle endowed, irrespective of factors such as intelligence or the conditions in which they are raised. Indeed, the converse case of possessing no language at all is so unusual that it is the exception which proves the rule.

The mentalist view of language is not only that language is a special mental property shared by all mankind, but that it is also particular to mankind, and not shared by other species on earth. Other species do, it is known, possess systems of communication, but as far as it has been possible to establish, these systems are limited in scope, and do not allow for 'innovation' and 'creativity' in the same way as human language does. Actually, there have been attempts, which have met with some limited degree of success, to school certain animals, such as chimpanzees, in human speech, but it is questionable whether such experiments really 'prove' anything beyond the fact that the higher orders among animals may share to some extent the characteristics of man; and this the theory of evolution already predicts. We can certainly say that no other species possesses the faculty of language to the same extent as human beings, and that there is a definite cut-off between humans and the very highest of other orders on the one hand and the rest of the animal kingdom on the other. What this in turn suggests is that the faculty of language is *innate*, and that no amount of stimulus-response training will bring it into being, even among animals which have articulatory organs similar to our own, if no basis for it exists to begin with.

Language acquisition and language learning

According to the behaviourist view of language, no greatly principled distinction is to be made between the learning of one's first, or native, language, and the learning of other languages at a later stage, since both would be seen in terms of stimulus-response training. The only real difference would be that the first language learnt would be likely to *interfere* with a second language being learnt (see Chapter Eleven). However, in the wake of Chomskyan linguistics, it has become axiomatic to distinguish between *acquisition* and *learning* and, whether or not one sees the learning of further languages as cases of acquisition or learning, certainly to tend to the view that the native language is acquired and not learnt. Firstly, 'learning' implies the making of a deliberate effort, of which in fact there is really no evidence in the case of a young child beginning to use the mother tongue. Secondly, 'learning' usually implies 'teaching', of which there is again little evidence, especially as parents respond to the content of what their children say rather than to the form in which they say it, and do not typically insist on repetition of 'word perfect' forms. Thirdly, children are exposed to language under vastly varying conditions of parental care, and this seems to make little difference in the end to the fact that they all acquire the system of their mother tongue. Again, the very enormity of what is involved in becoming competent in a language—coming to possess the potential ability to produce and understand *all* and *only* the sentences of a particular language—indicates that it could not be learnt in any normal sense of the term within the comparatively short time it takes for children to become competent speakers of their mother tongue. What is also interesting is that although children are exposed to many instances of 'degenerate', ungrammatical speech, they do not seem to absorb these instances into their own systems in such a way that they end up with no clear system themselves.

The mentalist view of first language acquisition as proposed by Chomsky is formalised in the Language Acquisition Device (LAD) Hypothesis. The LAD is not to be thought of as a particular part of the brain, or even as a physical entity at all, but as a special type of mental organisation, particular to human beings, which allows them to acquire language. All that is required to set the device into operation is exposure to language, and the device itself will then abstract from the instances of language fed into it the rules, or regularities, of the language in question; and the amassing together of this information about the rules of the language will come gradually, in successive stages, to constitute the individual's linguistic competence. The very fact that a child can distinguish—from birth, or even before, it would seem—between speech noises and other noises suggests that it is already endowed with some principled way of making the distinction. On the other hand, it cannot 'know' in advance which particular language it is going to be exposed to, so a corollary of the LAD hypothesis is that children are born with the equipment to acquire *any* human language, and that the process of acquiring a particular one involves some sort of 'filtering' or 'narrowing down' procedure. This is not so extraordinary as it may seem, since, beneath the surface, all human languages share a set of common characteristics, and are not arbitrarily different from each other. If the view represented here is correct, then, the acquisition of language in infancy is both pre-programmed and, given appropriate 'triggering', inevitable. Moreover, being 'automatic', it does not depend on motivation.

Of course, the foregoing should not be taken to suggest that there is nothing one can *learn* at all in relation to one's mother tongue, as it is quite obvious that one may come to gain conscious and explicit knowledge of some of its features in the course of education and life. However, though such conscious knowledge may later on affect the way one uses language, it is not the sort of knowledge required, or even accessible, to young children or even to many adults judged competent speakers of their language. Neither does it follow that simply because people possess linguistic competence they are good communicators—thus the LAD hypothesis itself does not, for example, mean that the study of the mother tongue as a school subject should now be viewed as redundant, even if it might suggest where some of the emphases in such a study should or should not lie. And, of course, it remains no more than a hypothesis, though an extremely influential one which has had a profound influence over the direction of research into child language acquisition in recent years.

Second language learning or acquisition?

Quite apart from the questions raised by the LAD hypothesis with regard to the mother tongue, it also raises significant questions where second or further languages are concerned. If the hypothesis is plausible with regard to the first language, should we assume that it provides insights into the mastering of other languages? Are second languages learnt, or should we now see them as being acquired? At present, there is no very clear answer to such questions. One complicating factor has been that some researchers have viewed puberty as a cut-off point for the functioning of the LAD. Certainly it is true that anyone not exposed to language at all prior to puberty seems incapable of acquiring it afterwards, which in itself suggests that the LAD 'packs up' after the first few years of life. Certainly also puberty always seems to represent a critical stage where language learning capability is concerned, and whether or not puberty is the correct place to draw the dividing line, it is now generally agreed that age is a most important factor in language learning in the sense that young children acquire foreign languages, at least under 'natural' conditions, in the same way as they acquire their mother tongue, whereas the position with regard to adults is much less certain (see Chapter Eleven for further discussion of this matter). So the question which is perhaps most important is: if the LAD hypothesis says something about the way in which children learn languages, whether first or subsequent, can it apply to the language learning of adults? Actually, it does seem to be the case that adults, immigrants into a country, perhaps, can simply 'pick up' a language without formal instruction on much the same basis as a child acquires the mother tongue, which in turn suggests that the LAD does not 'pack up' after the early years if it has already been put to use. However, we have to consider that adults, and perhaps older children, have developed their powers of conscious learning and their powers of control over what happens to them, and often appear able to utilise these powers to assist them in gaining mastery of foreign languages, so that to this extent they are learning rather than acquiring.

A recent psycholinguistic theory which purports to clarify the problem of learning versus acquisition with regard to adults is the so called *Monitor Model.* According to this theory, the adult language learner can *both* acquire and learn, that is, both 'pick up' and gain formal knowledge about languages. However, the performance of the adult as a language user depends, in terms of this theory, on what is in the acquired system, since it is the acquired system which is drawn upon in spontaneous speech. Conscious, formal knowledge, on the other hand, is not seen as a system which may be used for spontaneous performance, but may be used to 'monitor' and modify such performance, either before or after an utterance is actually made. There are certain conditions attaching to the use of the 'monitor': there must be time to use it; speakers must be conscious of the form of words they are going to use or have used, and not simply be concentrating on the content; and they must be fully aware of the 'rules' applying to the forms within their utterances. To boil this down to the essentials, adults will not become competent speakers of foreign languages unless they have been exposed to conditions in which they can 'absorb them into their systems' in the way that children do. If they only learn consciously, working through 'the rules', they may end up knowing a lot *about* a language, but they will not be able to perform fluently in it. Therefore, acquisition is indispensable to anyone who wants to actually speak a foreign language, and learning, though useful, is more of a luxury. This theory is controversial, and its critics are not satisfied, among other things, that it is possible to make a rigid distinction between acquisition and learning where adults are concerned, but it is already evident that it is having some impact on thought about foreign language teaching, to the extent that some specialists are now claiming that it is more or less a waste of time to insist on the learning of conscious rules, where the real task is to ensure that learners can acquire.

Language teaching

8 Teaching foreign languages

Describing what goes on in language teaching would be an impossible task if this meant giving an account of the procedures used by every language teacher everywhere. Ultimately, what happens in the language classroom is the product of the relationship between the particular teacher and the particular learners involved, and if we have any faith in the sensitivity and experience of teachers, this is how we would expect things to be. But the result is that in a certain sense there are as many methods of instruction as there are teachers, and the same teachers may vary their procedures frequently, depending upon the type of learners they are dealing with, the group dynamics of each class, the duration of the course, the availability of resources, and so on. It is also necessary to bear in mind, if we are trying to analyse any particular language teaching and language learning situation, that what goes on in the classroom may well vary from country to country in accordance with the current philosophy and policy of education, the social and political context, the economic climate, and perhaps many other factors which, though in principle unrelated to the technicalities of language teaching, influence both its content and its form. Nevertheless, while we cannot capture and describe all the details of language teaching in reality, we can discuss some of the major issues which in theory are universal and give an account of general trends in language teaching and the influences behind them.

Approach, technique and method
Since people sometimes learn foreign languages quite successfully without being taught in any conventional sense, it cannot be said

that teaching is always an absolutely necessary condition for learning. In practice, however, many, if not most, learners are first presented with a foreign language in circumstances in which teaching is taken for granted, or else seek teaching in one form or another. What is expected of language teachers, of course, is that they should make learning easier and more certain than it would be otherwise. Whether or not they actually do this probably depends more crucially on their general qualities as classroom teachers and on the relationships they develop with their students than on anything else, including the methods they use, but at the same time there are a number of decisions which have to be taken prior to the commencement of teaching which can influence the learning process considerably. These decisions include the syllabus to be followed, the texts to be used, the topics to be covered and the classroom activities to be engaged in. Decisions will also have to be made in the light of personality and cultural factors, and the age, experience and sophistication of the learners, on the manner of presentation, the sequencing of presentation and practice, the teaching pace to be adopted and the organisation of the classroom. Sometimes teachers make all such decisions autonomously, and sometimes they are made by central authorities such as ministries of education, but in all cases, the decisions, and the considerations leading to them, will reflect a general *approach* to the teaching of languages, that is to say, a general view of how language teaching should ideally be conducted. For example, it may be that the spoken language is regarded as the prime channel of communication in language, in which case the major emphasis will be placed upon it in teaching. On the other hand, the approach traditionally taken in school language teaching in Britain and elsewhere valued the written word above the spoken word, with the result that written language was the main focus of teaching. Again, it may be inherent in a certain approach to language teaching that learning through imitation and practice is the best way to learn a foreign language, while another approach may favour learning through the memorisation and subsequent application of rules of grammar. It is not necessarily always the case that a certain approach will be taken as the result of conscious deliberation on the principles involved; tradition can be a strong influence, and teaching is also subject to fashions.

The decisions made in the light of a certain approach to language teaching will have several practical outcomes. If one decides, for example, to teach by making students memorise and apply rules of grammar, then one will first have to identify, list and order the rules to be taught as teaching and learning points, and such an inventory of teaching and learning points will constitute the *syllabus* to be followed. The decision as to how to present the rules and make learners apply them will result in a set of teaching *techniques*. In the example we are considering, the techniques may include, firstly, an explanation of each rule to be given by the teacher in the mother tongue of the learners, secondly, the use of sentences in the mother tongue designed to be translated into the foreign language by the learners, applying the rules taught, and thirdly, correction of the learners' translations and, if necessary, renewed explanation of the rules. Techniques based on an oral approach to language teaching would usually be quite different, however, perhaps allowing for no explanation of rules and no use of the mother tongue, but encouraging much repetition and practice. Another decision about what is to be done in the classroom will concern *materials*. These may sometimes be highly formal, as in the case of textbooks which contain not only samples of the target language, but also exercises, summaries of grammatical rules and lists of vocabulary; but they can also be less formal, as when certain oral techniques are used which in effect 'generate' the materials round spontaneous discussion. Materials and teaching techniques interact with each other. Sometimes, when highly structured materials are used, the teaching techniques amount mainly to guiding the learners through the materials, while techniques employing less structured materials tend to demand more activity and ingenuity from the teacher. In some cases, materials may incorporate the teaching function entirely, as with many language courses for use at home which are structured in such a way as to make learners go through the procedures a teacher would normally put them through.

A set of teaching techniques, based on a certain type of syllabus and using certain types of materials, may be said to constitute a *method*; or, by circular definition, we may say that a method is the sum of teaching techniques utilised in a certain situation. As already mentioned, there is a sense in which there are as many methods as teachers, since the techniques teachers use will finally depend on the relationship between teachers and learners and the possibly unique conjunction of all other factors relevant to a given group of learners. However, there are various stereotyped methods which have been invented or developed over the course of time. In fact, there are probably dozens of methods with a distinctive name which are or have been advocated, but many of them tend to be variations on the same theme. It is perhaps worth outlining here some of the better-known, more established methods which are still in use in one form or another.

Grammar-Translation

Perhaps the method still most widely known among adults in the Western world is the *Grammar-Translation Method,* which is basically an adaptation of techniques used to teach classical languages. As its name implies, its cornerstones are the teaching of rules of grammar and translation of sentences and passages into the target language which prompt the use of the rules taught. Though not originally part of the method, its practitioners usually also advocate translation from the target language into the mother tongue. Texts for translation can in fact offer quite a rich semantic framework for language learning and up to a point the method ensures that learners are clear about the meaning of the language they are learning. Learners also generally acquire a good reading knowledge of the target language, and are accurate in their production of language if they have learnt conscientiously. However, as the method focuses on the written word, they tend not to cultivate oral fluency and spontaneity. Moreover, translation itself is a specialised skill, and not everyone wants to be a translator. Neither is it necessarily true that the best way of acquiring facility in a foreign language is through translation. The emphasis on creating a framework in which rules can be applied can also lead to stilted and unnatural use of language both by teachers and learners. Because the mother tongue is used to give explanations of the grammar taught, the method is clearly unsuitable for groups of mixed nationality or mother tongue.

Direct Method

Another well-known method, formulated in the latter part of the nineteenth century by a group of scholars and teachers who openly attacked the assumptions of Grammar-Translation, is the *Direct Method*. The approach underlying this saw speech rather than written language as the prime channel of communication to concentrate on, partly because speech was perceived as more universal than writing, and partly because children learn their mother tongue through speech and it was thought in consequence to be more 'natural' to acquire language orally. Translation was regarded not only as unnecessary to the acquisition of language, but as positively harmful, because it created difficulties which would not otherwise exist and provoked interference from the mother tongue. Indeed, seeking to compare two languages through translation was viewed as very dangerous for the beginner because learning a foreign language effectively was held to involve the learning of new and different thought-patterns, not just learning how to graft foreign vocabulary onto the thought-patterns of the mother tongue culture. Learning a foreign language, then, meant learning a new and independent system of language, but it also meant becoming immersed in the culture of the target language, and the Direct Method sought to encourage interest in the foreign culture. In this method, which is still in use, all material to be learnt is first—and in the initial stages, exclusively—presented orally in the target language, grammar being taught not through rules but by situation and association. Learners are required to engage in much repetition of what the teacher says until they have acquired a certain grammatical pattern, which they then vary in further practice. Presentation without translation or use of the mother tongue necessitates complex procedures for conveying meaning, and the axiom that the mother tongue should not be used at all, even though this could be the most efficient solution to some problems, has sometimes tended to become a rather unnecessary fetish. The strong point of this method is that learners cultivate oral fluency and spontaneity, but one of its weak points is that it does not impart any real grammatical 'awareness', so that it is often difficult for learners to tackle new material on their own.

Audiolingualism

It should be apparent that the differences between the two methods discussed so far reflect different views not only on linguistic but also on psychological and sociological matters. The process of language learning is conceived of in different ways, the Grammar-Translation Method assuming that thought should go into the process, with conscious memorisation of rules, and the Direct Method assuming that the learning of a language is basically the acquisition of new speech habits and new thought-patterns associated with the culture of the target language. However, though both methods reflect views on the nature of language and of learning, these views are in a sense informal, since they do not proceed from a totally systematic body of knowledge. The third method we shall discuss has a somewhat, different basis, since it claimed to be consistent with the formal principles of linguistics and psychology. This is the *Audio-Lingual Method*, which reached the height of its popularity in the late 1950s and early 1960s. It was inspired in part by an earlier method, called *Mimicry-Memorisation*, which had been used, apparently with great success, in the language training of American military personnel in the Second World War, and was based on an approach to language eaching similar to that underlying the Direct Method. However, under the influence of behaviourist psychology, the concept of a language as a habit system, which could be accounted for in terms of stimulus-response conditioning, was now much more formal, and it was held that learning a habit system of this kind was a formidable task. In order to make learning efficient, the points to be taught might be arrived at by the process of *contrastive analysis*, which involves direct comparison between the phonological and phonetic, grammatical and semantic aspects of two different languages—in this case the learner's mother tongue and the target language—in order to determine the major points of divergence between them. The assumption was that these major differences would represent the most difficult learning points since they would mark the greatest discrepancies between the system of habits established in learners by their mother tongue and the new system of habits to be acquired, and would by the same token be the points at which the risk of interference from the mother tongue would be highest. The techniques of analysis used to determine the syllabus were provided by American structuralist linguistics, which assumed that the structures of a language could be looked upon as a system of sentence patterns. Once the sentence patterns to be taught were identified, the requirement from behaviourist psychology was that they be ingrained in the learner through *drilling*, and the *pattern drill*, an exercise in which learners manipulate the sentence patterns of the target language until they can produce them 'automatically', became established as a major technique. The method also, however, owes much to the theory of programmed instruction, which breaks learning down into minimal steps which are ordered in terms of complexity. It should also be noted that Audiolingualism claimed the skills of language to be Listening, Speaking, Reading, Writing—to be taught and learnt in that order. Though some efforts were made to provide a context for the patterns drilled in class, it turned out in practice that 'withdrawal of meaning' owing to insufficient contextualisation proved a serious problem—learners could often chant drills impeccably, but all too frequently did not really understand what they were saying and could not apply the structures rehearsed in meaningful contexts. It was also an axiom of Audiolingualism in its 'pure' form that, by contrast with Mimicry-Memorisation, explanations of grammar should not be provided even if requested, and this did nothing to assist the learner hopelessly lost with regard to meaning. Moreover, contrastive analysis did not in fact pinpoint all the difficulties; learners made unpredicted errors and sometimes did not make the ones predicted. Later, error analysis, linked with the interlanguage hypothesis, produced a more reliable way of predicting what will happen when a learner moves from one language to the other. Audiolingualism finally came in for savage criticism on theoretical grounds when, principally under the influence of the American linguist Chomsky, both behaviourist psychology and structuralist linguistics were argued to be based on untenable views. Audiolingualism suffered from having claimed support from these sources, and many teachers, having once been told that Audiolingualism was founded on 'scientific principles', became disillusioned and suspicious of theorists.

In fact a number of useful lessons came out of the experience with Audiolingualism. The first was that teachers should not tie themselves too closely to theorists, whether linguists or psychologists, but while being prepared to accept suggestions, should determine classroom procedures on the basis of their practical expertise and their knowledge of their students' needs. Many teachers using the Audio-Lingual Method admitted to 'subverting' it by adapting and modifying its techniques where they judged this appropriate. This is in the end the only sensible approach to adopt, and it is precisely because teachers adapt techniques so regularly that it is difficult to find instances of well-known, established methods being used in 'pure' form. Another lesson which was clearly brought home during this period was that there is no such thing as a 'best' method. In retrospect, it is somewhat surprising that anyone should ever have thought there could be such a thing, but the specialist literature is full of claims which amount to saying that this or that method is 'best', and it was once believed by some that there must in principle be a 'global' method, that is, one for universal application, responding to pretty well all language teaching and learning problems. Costly experiments were even conducted with the aim of showing the superiority of the Audio-Lingual Method over more traditional procedures, but though the experiments did not really succeed as such, they produced enough evidence to underline the obvious—that students trained by oral methods tend, at least initially, to be better in oral work, and those trained by methods focusing on the written word tend, at least initially, to be better in reading and writing. The third lesson follows from the second: methods reflect implicit *aims.* Much of the argument about 'best' methods becomes vacuous once this is acknowledged, so long as we accept that it is legitimate for people to differ with regard to the aims they have in learning a language. If someone wishes above all to speak a language with facility, then the obvious thing is for that person to be taught by a method which stresses spoken language, and if someone wishes above all to read and write a language, then the obvious thing is for that person to be taught by a method, such as Grammar-Translation, which aims primarily to teach facility in the written language. It is then, ideally speaking, putting the cart before the horse for a teacher to start off by deciding which method to use; the first concern should be to establish exactly what teaching and learning are to aim at, and then to choose a method, or techniques from various methods, accordingly. Notwithstanding these latter remarks, the fourth lesson we should mention here, which again began to emerge fairly clearly from the experiments comparing Audiolingualism with other methodologies, is that a method itself is unlikely to be such a critical factor in success or failure as might have been supposed. It would in fact seem preferable for teachers to employ methods they can handle with confidence, even if such methods are not ideally suited to the situation, than to lose control over their teaching and demotivate their students by using techniques they are uncomfortable with. At least all methods share the virtue of arranging for the exposure of the learner to the target language.

Communicative approaches

A feature to note about methods as developed up to the time of Audiolingualism is that by and large they presuppose that the structural, or strictly linguistic, aspects of the target language pose the greatest problem to the learner. This also seemed to be the presupposition of attempts to come up with new methodologies—most notably those based on Cognitive Code-Learning Theory and 'Nativism'—in the backlash against Audiolingualism and in the light of Chomskyan linguistics. However, both social pressures and evidence from sociolinguistic research have in recent times led to approaches emphasising not linguistic competence as the goal for language teaching so much as *communicative competence*. Sociolinguistic studies have prompted more detailed examination than in the past of the way people interact with each other and of the kind of language they use to accomplish various things. It has become apparent, for instance, that there is no straightforward relationship between grammatical categories and *functions* of language—between, say, the category 'interrogative' and the function 'asking questions', since native speakers can in fact elicit information as much through statements as through questions. How often, for example, does one ask the way by actually asking? We can just as easily signal our request for information by saying something like: 'Excuse me, I'm rather lost ... I was looking for the station.' Learning to use language appropriately and learning to engage not simply in speech but in *speech acts* means, then, mastering more than just the structures of a language, and indeed, more than the language itself; in the final analysis it also means learning how to *behave* in a certain culture, and to this extent one must acknowledge that the founders of the Direct Method were right to insist on the cultural connection. As a result of the work on the analysis of interaction, syllabuses aiming at communicative competence no longer concentrate so much on grammar but look at the nature of meaning and of interactions. Syllabuses of this kind are usually referred to as 'functional' or 'notional' or 'functional-notional'. These issues are discussed in greater detail in Chapter Fourteen.

While language teaching has taken account of the notion of communicative competence, it has also responded in recent years to pressures to integrate aspects of the learner's personality more fully into the the learning process. Indeed, what seems to underlie certain new approaches is the idea that learning a foreign language is, almost more than anything else, a question of overcoming psychological inhibitions and emotional problems so that one can bring one's inherent intellectual resources fully into play. To some extent this development has been reinforced by demand, especially from adult learners, for teaching in small groups in which individual problems can be given special attention. This general trend is sometimes referred to as 'whole-person learning' and the procedures developed are also sometimes termed 'humanistic techniques' by their proponents, though this implies a somewhat arrogant dismissal of a long tradition of foreign language teaching which in many countries has made a prime contribution to humanistic education. The techniques themselves often reflect elements of counselling and drama-therapy, and stress co-operation between learners rather than competition. As distinct methods which fall broadly into this category one might mention three which have been widely publicised. The first is The Silent Way, developed in the United States by Gattegno, which perhaps above all aims to encourage learners to utilise their own inner resources as fully as possible. Another is Community Language Learning, again developed in the United States, by Curran, which fosters co-operation and high personal involvement in the task of learning. The third is Suggestopedia, pioneered in Bulgaria by Lozanov, which might again be said to bring out the hidden resources of the learner by creating conditions under which total commitment to learning is possible. There are in fact few features of 'whole-person learning' techniques which cannot be tried in large classrooms with children and adolescents in state education, but it is unlikely that the techniques in themselves can provide all the answers to the problems of conventional classes. However, the fact that such techniques have in some quarters met an enthusiastic response suggests that dissatisfaction with conventional procedures should be examined and that perhaps not enough is done to acknowledge the total personality of learners and to supply the motivational support often needed. It is certainly easy within state education for language teaching to come across as cold, dry and dull. It is the duty of teachers to avoid this, of course, and one of the ways in which they can best prepare themselves to do so is by keeping up with new developments and trying out new techniques in their own classes.

Apart from the possible tendency to neglect the total personality of the learner, perhaps the most discouraging feature of traditional school language teaching has been its negative and often highly punitive attitude towards error, an attitude to be explained by the fact that it has operated *norm-referenced* criteria. This is to say that utterances of learners have been judged in terms of the linguistic norms maintained by educated adult native speakers of the target language, and deviations from these norms have been treated as evidence of failure to learn properly. However, as already mentioned in the chapter on psychology, there is now reason to believe that the natural psychological processes of foreign language learning may be very similar to those of first language learning, to the extent that both mother tongue learners and foreign language learners approach the language through a series of successive systems approximating more and more closely to it. Consequently, it has been suggested not only that systematic error in foreign language learning is useful as an indication of progress, but that learners must make, and must be allowed to make, errors in order to develop models of the target language for them to exploit themselves. Moreover, once one begins to make an analogy between first and foreign language learning, it becomes clear that first and foreign language learners are usually subjected to dual standards. Our concern with young children learning the mother tongue is that they should develop fluency and be at home in using the language to accomplish things—that they should, in short, be capable of engaging in speech acts. We are prepared to be patient, and to wait for them to develop language conforming to the linguistic norms of adults. With foreign language learners we have traditionally had little patience in this respect; we have not given much credit, either, for attempts to accomplish speech acts with whatever linguistic resources learners possess, even though similar attempts by mother tongue learners often delight teachers. Thus, wherever fluency and ease in production of the target language are among the aims of language teaching, the analogy between first and foreign language learning would seem to have a clear implication: that learners should be helped to put their linguistic resources to use in meaningful contexts in order to develop fluency and ease. This would mean that, while it is still necessary to feed in a model of the target language in socially-valued form, linguistic error should be regarded as an integral part of language learning development. For this to happen, the classroom must become a language-using community in which learners can themselves experiment with the language and are encouraged to use it to communicate what they genuinely want to communicate, however inadequately at first. In short, language teaching needs to incorporate many more exercises and activities in which success is judged less in terms of linguistic norms and more in terms of the total efficacy with which tasks using language are performed; it should, then, operate *performance-referenced* criteria. Plainly, though the motivation for the arguments referred to here is different, they are linked with those surrounding communicative competence as a goal of language teaching.

Teaching languages for special, or specific, purposes

Teaching languages for special purposes, or for specific purposes, as some specialists prefer to say, is an important sub-branch of language teaching about which we should add a few words. Though not an entirely new idea, it is only in recent years that it has taken on an identity of its own. In relation to English, it is usually referred to as 'ESP' (ee-ess-pee), and further sub-categories within it usually come to be designated by a similar type of acronym, for example, 'EAP' (ee-ay-pee)—English for Academic Purposes. One of its most important branches is 'EST' (ee-ess-tee)—English for Science and Technology.

The development of special-purpose language teaching is due to the combination of at least two major factors: the increasing pressure to teach languages quickly and efficiently, especially to busy adults who require a language for the expansion and enhancement of their careers, and the emergence, from research in linguistics, sociolinguistics and applied linguistics, of potential ways of doing this. In essence, the 'special-purpose approach' is the communicative approach carried to its logical conclusion. If we set out to teach for communication, then we can ask in relation to any learner or group of learners what the *communicative needs* of this person or these people are and, if we can identify the needs, we can make them the priorities in both the syllabus and the teaching. In this way, we can aim only to teach those parts of the language and its use which are relevant, and depart from the traditional notion that to make a fluent speaker we have to teach the 'whole' of the language. Prior to the theory of communicative competence and work on functional and notional syllabuses, striving after efficiency in this manner was far more difficult because there was no principled way of relating the language to the purposes it was required for. Now, however, we can ask what speech-acts a person needs to perform in the language to be learnt, what skills involving the use of language will be required, what functions these speech-acts and skills entail and finally what *linguistic* exponents, that is, actual vocabulary and structures, these functions necessitate. At the same time, of course, we can take into account any specialised vocabulary and structures involved in the subject-areas pertinent to the learners' activities. Having identified the needs, we can compare them with what the learner already knows, and can already do in the target language, and 'trim down' to the basic teaching requirements. From this description, it will be seen that *needs-analysis* is central to special purpose language teaching, but we are bound to add that although the procedures as outlined here may sound straightforward, needs-analysis is in fact a difficult task involving many complexities. Not the least of these are that there can be conflicts of interest between bodies funding language courses, such as employers, and other parties concerned, including the learners. Again, it often emerges that needs as identified in advance of a course do not coincide with needs as identified while the course is ongoing; that needs are in a sense dynamic and changing rather than static, and that some sort of review procedure needs to be built into courses.

Special-purpose language teaching has brought with it a great interest in and concern with *register analysis* (see Chapter Five), that is, analysis of the language appropriate to particular areas of interest, for example the 'language of science'. Obviously, if it can be established that particular areas have their own 'language', this will increase the potential specificity of teaching. However, results so far have been only tentative, and precision difficult, because while particular areas may have preferred forms and styles, these are not compulsory, and are not consistently maintained by all engaged in each field.

It seems unlikely that special-purpose language teaching will greatly affect what is done in schools, especially with younger children, since it is really only adults who can have clearly identifiable communicative needs. By contrast with special purpose courses, school-type language courses are nowadays often referred to as 'general purpose' courses. However, there is no doubt some room for a more careful consideration of the communicative needs of older school pupils in particular, and the special-purpose approach would exert a healthy influence on school language teaching if it led to a greater concern with ensuring that the language taught at school was as appropriate as possible to the age and interests of pupils, as well as to a greater concern with what pupils could actually *do* in a foreign language.

Individualisation in language learning

Even a brief account of foreign language learning and teaching must make some reference to individualisation, which in recent years has become an increasingly important approach to the organisation of language learning. Actually, the concept of individualisation is by no means confined to the learning and teaching of foreign languages; it is equally applicable in mother tongue teaching and, indeed, in the teaching of any subject, but it is in relation to foreign language instruction that it seems to have attracted particular attention. What individualisation amounts to is the creation of a learning and teaching environment in which the individual needs, abilities and interests of each learner are fully taken into account, where possible to the extent of allowing individual programmes of learning with regard to *objectives, pace of learning, methods* and *content of materials.* Individualisation is, then, the converse of the more traditional approach to learning and teaching, which assumes that the class should be 'kept together', and that the teacher should 'aim for the middle'. It is fundamental to the philosophy of individualisation that learning rather than teaching is the essential activity of the classroom, that learners should ultimately be responsible for their own learning, and that the teacher should be perceived as a facilitator or manager of learning rather than as a purveyor of knowledge. This does not actually relieve the teacher of any responsibility; if anything, it increases it, since it is undoubtedly more difficult to manage many individual learning programmes than to orchestrate a class round a common syllabus.

Undoubtedly, one of the reasons why individualisation has become a more popular idea in recent years is that it is very much easier to put into practice now that a wide range of technological aids to learning and teaching is available (see Chapter Thirteen for further discussion of this point). However, its practicability does not rest entirely on the availability of technological aids, but much more on the willingness of the teacher to individualise to whatever degree is possible, given the resources at hand. In this connection, it is important to bear in mind that individualisation is not an 'all or nothing' enterprise: there are degrees and degrees of it. It may not be possible to allow for a range of different objectives—one learner learning French for purposes of tourism, another in order to read French history and another in order to execute business correspondence in French, for example—because, perhaps, somewhere in the distance a school leaving examination is looming up which permits no such range of choices; but at least it might be possible to allocate some class-time to the pursuit of these different interests under the heading 'content of materials' by building in a 'free stage' during which learners read or write whatever appeals to them. It cannot be denied that thoroughgoing individualisation is expensive in terms of time and materials and resources, but ingenuity on the part of the teacher, and the willingness to permit learners to follow up their own interests at least occasionally, costs little in monetary terms, and is probably one of the best ways to ensure that motivation is maintained. Certainly, teachers faced with so called 'mixed ability' classes would do well to consider how and to what extent they might individualise, or they will end up with some very dissatisfied 'customers' at one or the other end of the ability range.

We must still remember, of course, that as language teaching and learning can have a variety of different aims and be conducted in many different situations, nothing said here is intended to represent a general prescription. While it may be appropriate to generalise that language teachers should be systematic, well organised, sympathetic and good motivators, when it comes to choosing techniques, the last thing they should do is simply chase fashion. Only specific circumstances can guide the selection of techniques from among the wide range available.

9 Teaching the mother language

Approaches to teaching the mother tongue vary enormously from country to country, and there is scarcely any agreement about what is appropriate activity for a mother tongue class. There are a number of reasons for this. First, mother tongue teaching embraces two distinct traditions: the study of literature, deriving ultimately from the study of classical literature, and the study of language, deriving mainly from attempts to teach the standard language as a second dialect to allegedly non-standard speakers. The second tradition, particularly, has not usually been defined in these terms, but it is noteworthy that discussion of how to 'teach' the English language only arose when education became compulsory for all classes and groups. Linked to this tradition, of course, has been the issue of teaching writing in the standard language, and here it links with the classical tradition, where the development of a 'good' prose style was a major aim. Nonetheless, discussion of mother tongue teaching poses for us a large number of educational and sociolinguistic problems (and indeed a number of social and political ones) which can be avoided when we are simply looking at foreign language learning and teaching. Yet, when we look closely, we can see that the two cannot be separated completely from each other. In nearly all countries there are minorities who may have to learn the language of the majority as a second language, with psychological and methodological implications relating the process to foreign language work, but with economic and sociological aspects relating it to mother tongue issues. It is very difficult to distinguish totally between, for example, Catalan speakers learning Castilian Spanish, Welsh or Gujarati speakers learning English, Swiss German speakers learning

German or French, or speakers of English from Devon learning standard spoken English. In each of these cases similar problems have to be faced, for in each case the speaker is being asked to move from the language or dialect of home to one which has wider currency. There will often be difficulties in doing this, but the extent of these difficulties will depend on factors like the closeness of the original language or culture to the target one, the value of the target culture as seen by the learner, the degree of parental support, the attitude taken by central government to the original language, and similar considerations which may be political and economic.

Sociolinguistic studies make it clear that, in respects like these, mother tongue teaching must increasingly recognise diversity in the schools, and must therefore, at the very least, concede that it has some similarity with foreign and second language teaching. And conversely, much of the work of mother tongue teachers has great relevance to foreign language teaching.

Yet, although it is possible to generalise about all the social groups mentioned previously, members of these groups would see their own situations as very different from those of other groups. The similarities should not blur the major differences between the various cultures involved, for one reason for the many different approaches to mother tongue teaching is precisely these differences. Different countries—indeed different areas within countries—take differing approaches to education, to language, and to children. On the whole, foreign language teaching has been seen essentially as a technical problem for teachers to overcome, but mother tongue teaching has more often been seen as intimately bound up with cultural values. Teachers have therefore been less willing to concentrate on technical solutions to their problems. Their attitude to the 'scientific' claims of linguistics has been suspicious and no other theoretical discipline has won universal acceptance as a basis for language work. Literary criticism, sociology, psycho-analysis, politics and linguistics have all had their advocates, but none of them alone can provide the basis for a theory of mother tongue teaching.

Why, then, do we include a chapter on mother tongue teaching in a book such as this? Partly because, if linguistics is indeed the scientific study of language, it must have something to say about the mother tongue, for that is the natural form which language takes. It would be a poor study if it could only talk about the relatively unusual situation of formal education for the learning of foreign languages.

And partly because there is a great danger of mother tongue teaching claiming a unique relationship with politics, sociology and so on. The issues raised by teaching the mother tongue in relation to these other disciplines are also raised by other school subjects, though of course in slightly different ways. Some of them relate to issues concerning the nature of a common culture, some to the role of self-expression in education, some to the acquisition of a specialised language for a formal discipline. None of these problems is unique to mother tongue teaching. But the central issue with the mother tongue is the nature of language, and this of course is the concern of linguistics.

We have seen in Chapter Eight how many basic linguistic procedures have been adapted to foreign language classrooms. It is worth noting that in British mother tongue teaching in the past a very similar approach was adopted, and there are schools and countries where it is still held that fairly rigid exercises in the standard language should be taught in a highly formal way. Teachers have, indeed, been known to insist that 'correct' (i.e. standard) forms are 'a foreign language' to their students, or that the written language is a foreign mode to any illiterate speaker of the language. It is clear, though, that any discussion along these lines presupposes answers to several basic questions. Perhaps the best way of charting our way through the maze of approaches would be to address these fundamental questions separately.

Mother tongue 'improvement'

There can be no justification for teaching the mother tongue in schools if it is not believed that improvement is thereby made possible in its use. Any kind of teaching presupposes that there is some view of increased competence in the abilities being developed. So, by definition, pupils learning their mother tongue will end up using it differently from the way they use it at the beginning. Also, because of the close connection between language and cultural grouping which has been referred to several times earlier in this book, the ways in which teachers help students to develop linguistically will have significant social and political implications. At the same time, because of this close connection with culture, there will be major linguistic changes taking place which the teacher and educational system can accompany but not control. There is little point in devoting massive energy to the maintenance of a mother tongue unless there is a strong economic or political motivation for students to retain it. Nor is there much point in continuing to teach a language simply because it has always been taught. During periods of strong nationalist fervour, national languages frequently develop strongly; but usually there needs to be some fairly major economic or political justification for retaining national ties if the language is to continue to develop. English is in a peculiar position, for—by a combination of historical accidents—it has achieved a position of economic domination in the world, and is thus more in demand than any other foreign language. One consequence of this is that English reflects more and more a whole range of different cultural aspirations and assumptions. Another is that the teaching of English is rarely on the defensive. But for other mother tongues, the situation may be very different. The learning of (for example) Gujarati, or Welsh, or Italian, as a mother tongue in Britain is a serious political issue at the moment, and every other country has similar minority languages to consider. Each situation is different, and has to be assessed in terms of the extent of local demand, the amount of money available for development of teaching materials, training of teachers, etc., the political implications, particularly the risks of creating isolated and politically disfranchised sub-groups, the existence of an extensive literature in the mother tongue, and so on. It is not simply a matter of saying that everyone has a right to mother tongue maintenance, for there are many very difficult sociolinguistic problems to resolve. Is Italian a mother tongue? Or should we teach Neapolitan to Neapolitans, Sicilian to Sicilians and so on? Where should such subdividing stop? Indeed, if one proceeds far enough on this line, it is difficult to see how any teaching could be justified at all, for we should simply confirm each speaker in his own speech. Ultimately, the solution to problems of this kind can only be based on a careful appraisal of each case separately, together with a clear view of the purpose of mother tongue teaching.

What is that purpose? A large number of different ones have been suggested at different times. However, certain general trends may be distinguished. Most mother tongue teaching concerns itself—to a great extent—with the promotion of literacy and oracy, the former being concerned with reading and writing, and the latter with effective oral activity. Although there has been a fashion in recent years to argue that literacy is an outmoded idea, no-one has yet developed a cheaper or more adaptable way of transmitting a lot of material than a book, and for a long time people who are skilled readers and writers will have an advantage over those who are not. For this reason there is a strong democratic justification for attempting to ensure that all citizens are able to read and write fluently, in order not to be exploited. At the same time, of course, people do need to be able to operate effectively as speakers and listeners as well—and, indeed, effective speaking and listening may be a good way of developing effective reading and writing. So schools in Britain particularly have, in the last twenty years or so, placed heavy emphasis on the development of oral skills. This has not been simply to assist language development in the abstract, for it is widely believed that the process of discussing what has to be learnt, in all subjects, is a major factor in successful learning. And this, of course, fits in with our discussion of the relationship between language development and concept development.

There are other abilities to be developed, however, though they will not be developed exclusively through language work. Much mother tongue teaching has concerned itself with learning about literature, sometimes as an end in itself, but more often as a way of developing critical and analytical abilities. There is of course an argument, though it is not a very popular one now, for simply introducing students, through literature, to the tradition of classical writing of their language, and a great deal of teaching in Britain still assumes that there are major works which all students should read and major authors whom all students should know about. But it is more often argued that reading works of literature has a value in itself—though when we look carefully at the arguments, the value is usually seen as psychological, social or political rather than purely literary. It is certainly true, however, that the ability to read with discrimination is a necessary one, both for an appreciation of literature, and for participation in the modern world, so—at the higher levels of teaching—there is a happy identification between the demands of the subject and the social needs of the community.

But this takes us some way from language teaching, for the study of literature, and indeed the study of language—linguistics—are quite different activities from the improvement of abilities to use a language, whether mother tongue or foreign. We need to note, though, that there is always a tendency, because of the apparent absence of content in language teaching, for teachers to move towards content areas, such as literature, linguistics, or—in the overseas situation—the teaching of culture. All of these may assist language development, but knowledge in each of these areas does not constitute ability to use the language effectively. However, it is difficult to conceive of 'using the language effectively' without some notion of what it is being used for, so questions of content and function still have some relevance.

It may be helpful to think of mother tongue teaching first of all in terms of minimum capacities. As is not the case with many school subjects, a basic competence in the mother tongue is essential. People survive quite satisfactorily without any knowledge of physics or natural history or geography, and may lead fulfilled lives taking an interest in activities which do not appear in the school curriculum at all. But, as with basic numeracy, not to be able to read, write and talk appropriately to people from various groups in society (and not only officials) is to be hindered in the options available. However difficult it is to define basic literacy, we all know more or less what it means, and a school system which sends out students unable to operate in the official language of the country (which is usually the mother tongue of most of the inhabitants) creates political and social instability. All normal students, therefore, should be able to read effectively any material which is likely to come the way of all citizens, should be able to write well enough to deal with all normal personal and public situations, and should be able to talk confidently enough not to be afraid of any normal conversation. It is necessary to state this straightforwardly, like this, for such elementary points are often neglected. A school system which does not offer these essentials is stealing life-chances from its pupils.

But of course this is only a minimum. There are many important needs for language beyond these. We have already referred to literature teaching, which can be treated in many ways as a separate subject, but advanced work in any area makes linguistic demands upon students, while they have personal needs in language which ultimately merge with those of further academic work and those of society. How best to relate linguistic needs with broader educational ones is a subject of constant debate, and—because of the far more complicated role of mother tongue teaching (it is central where foreign language teaching is peripheral)—there is very little consensus. Indeed, there is a tendency for English departments in Britain, in their search for relevant subject matter for language development, to take on almost the whole of moral and political education. This need not matter, and it has been the stimulus for a great deal of interesting work, providing the minimum requirements of literacy and oracy are not sacrificed to either of the two extremes: the view that 'we have no right to improve their English' on the one hand is incompatible with any view of education, while the view that English is 'really' about developing literary appreciation, on the other, substitutes a perfectly valid subject for the quite different, and more basic, need to develop ability to use the language in varied and appropriate situations.

What has the role of linguistics been in all this? At a technical level, there have been major contributions to our understanding of the processes of early language learning, of the development of initial literacy, and of advanced comprehension. Discussion of these areas, though, has usually reached teachers at second hand, and references in the bibliography will provide guidance on further reading for those who are interested. Since the early days of mass education, particularly in the United States, there has been considerable interest in descriptive models of language used directly in the classroom. However, there is a risk that the ability to describe the language becomes confused with the ability to use it, and there is no direct evidence to support the view that those who can discuss the grammar are more effective writers than those who cannot. At the same time, many students really enjoy talking about the language, and there is no reason why this should be discouraged. There are good arguments for the teaching of elementary linguistics in schools—but they are not arguments which bear directly on the improvement of standards of literacy. The most important linguistic influences in recent years have been sociolinguistic. Our understanding of the variety and flexibility of language makes us more sympathetic than in the past to the variety of languages present (as well as the varieties of language) in any one school. This is particularly necessary as Britain becomes more and more a multicultural society, but is also so to some extent in schools in all countries.

It has frequently been asserted—and linguists bear some responsibility for this view—that all languages are equally 'good' or 'valid'. Now this assertion immediately becomes nonsense if we ask 'good for what?' It is probably true (though impossible to prove or demonstrate) that all languages can potentially be used for all possible purposes, and it is certainly true that there are no languages which are demonstrably simple or primitive in structure. But it is certainly also true that a language which has never been used for writing customarily organises itself to assist oral memory in a way in which one which is frequently written does not. A language which has developed many terms for use in the mountains of northern Europe may be ill-equipped for dealing with activity in tropical jungles or deserts. Languages, that is to say, reflect the cultures in which they have been used, and there are always difficulties in translating from one culture to another, even within one language, let alone across from one to another. The point is that linguists need to accept that we do not want to interpret one language as a failed version of another, so, in describing languages, we should assume that 'all languages are equal'. But this is a methodological axiom, not a statement of observed fact, and education has to be based on the assumption that some linguistic forms have wider currency than others, that certain forms are more useful for particular purposes — in other words that there are linguistic conventions which we must learn to recognise, even if eventually we may want to break them for our own purposes. Furthermore, it is necessary for us to recognise that this process of development and change in the language we use is entirely natural. There is no linguistic form which is 'good' for all purposes, no item of vocabulary which is absolutely better than another. But there are forms which are inappropriate in certain contexts—that is to say that they are wrong, because they convey a meaning which will be misunderstood. Variations in formality are variations in meaning, as we saw in Chapter Four. If we want to be offensive to someone in authority by addressing him too informally, then there will be no misunderstanding, but we must recognise that a rule is deliberately being broken. A pupil who addresses someone in authority very informally and is rude by mistake, rather than on purpose, has produced the wrong language for the situation. And this principle applies even though there are problems in defining appropriate behaviour to those in authority. We may possibly think that those in authority should not be addressed formally, and it may be that such usage will disappear if enough people come to agree with us, but until that has happened the rule will still exist, and not to recognise its existence is to misunderstand the rules of the language.

It is important to emphasise this point, for there has been a tendency among some mother tongue teachers to claim that movement towards standard language is in some sense a middle class conspiracy. It is possible, of course, that the advantages of being brought up surrounded by standard English will be exploited by those who have enjoyed them, but the tendency to standardise, for the language to become more widely intelligible, is an inevitable product of people needing to talk with each other across a wide range of geographical regions and social backgrounds. Insofar as we share a common culture, we shall come to share a common dialect; insofar as, being individuals, we will hold our own local and individual identities, we shall use language subtly distinct from the common dialect. But we are all multi-dialectal, and only those who live in a totally isolated community, with a continuity of interest for decades on end, will produce unvaried language. Insofar as schools emancipate and broaden horizons they will extend and enlarge linguistic repertoires: the two processes are inseparable.

Language and culture

This issue becomes particularly important when we consider the role of reading and writing. There are certainly some sections of the community where reading is less central to life than in others. It may well be, though again it has not and perhaps cannot be conclusively proved, that children from non-reading families are at a disadvantage, not merely when learning to read but also when engaged on any kind of educated discourse in schools. There have been claims, particularly in the early work of the sociologist Basil Bernstein, that the recognised lack of success—comparatively—of working class children in academic education may be accounted for by a fundamental mismatch between the language of the home and the language of the school. Over-simple reactions to this suggestion (and note that, plausible as it may sound, it has not been proved) have been arguments that schools should 'become working class institutions' or that 'schools should provide language classes in standard English as a second dialect'. Both of these suggestions ignore the close relationship between language and culture. *If* there is an incompatibility between being academic, literate and working class (and there is no evidence to sugggest that there is), then schools will either have to stop having anything to do with being academic and literate, and hence to do with education at all as we know it, pupils or will have to be socialised away from their class origins in order to be educated. However, there is massive evidence to support the view that working class access to the standard language does not prevent class identification. The problem only arises because the questions are wrongly phrased. Schools do represent a common culture, and will to some extent reflect that in a tendency to emphasise the common language. There will always be some groups in society whose interests will coincide more or less closely with those of schools, and whose children will consequently be relatively advantaged. There is no way of avoiding this without depriving parents of freedom of manoeuvre in the ways they bring up their children. But there is no one working class culture, there are many different ones in different regions of the country. There is no common middle class culture, and both classes have values which conflict with education as well as ones which support it. The much more interesting problem, and the one to which Bernstein's more recent work has addressed itself, is how to separate what is essential in educational development from what is merely conventional. What principles establish what is considered to be legitimate knowledge? It may be a sociolinguistic fact (and an undesirable one) that many people, including teachers, judge people's intelligence by the way they speak, but this is unimportant compared with the question of how language work in school can help children to develop their intellectual and imaginative capacities to the highest level. And, indeed, the impact of sociolinguistic research has made teachers more sensitive to language variation. Most mother tongue teachers now would insist on observation of straightforward conventions in writing, but expect pupils to be able to express themselves effectively in their own speech, without attempts to change accent and dialect forms towards a prescribed norm.

A good mother tongue class, then, will help children develop their own use of language, through creative writing, project work and group activities which involve a lot of pupil-pupil talk as well as pupil-teacher talk. It will also make sure that all children are able to produce appropriate writing in all areas in which writing may be demanded by society, and able to read whatever may be demanded of them by society. The former aspect centres on the child's personal needs, and the latter on society's. Both aspects, as in any teaching, need to be taken into account. Later work will develop an interest in reading for its own sake, probably developing out of stories told to, and by, children in their early years, and leading on to the study of literature on a more formal basis. This may branch out into integrated studies relating to drama, consideration of film and television and discussion of political and sociological questions arising out of reading and as a basis for personal writing. In some schools, this may lead on to formal study of language or of literature as academic disciplines.

Thus, compared with foreign language teaching, there will be more emphasis in the mother tongue class on work for the personal development of the student. But institutional or social linguistic demands should not be ignored, any more than personal demands should in the foreign language class. On the whole, foreign language classrooms have traditionally been much clearer than mother tongue ones in specifying objectives and designing explicit syllabuses. There are good reasons for mother tongue teachers not to be too explicit in advance about what they are going to do, but the two groups of teachers have more to learn from each other than is usually realised.

10 Teaching second languages

Most of what needs to be said under this heading can be related closely to the content of the two previous chapters, for second language work fits uneasily in between foreign language and mother tongue work. To express the relationship a little over-simply, second language learning involves the psychological problems of foreign languages coupled with the sociological situation of the mother tongue.

There are two basic situations of second language teaching. One is in a country where there are substantial numbers of people who do not speak the official language of education and national life. This may be because they have recently immigrated or because they have been brought up in a long-standing community speaking a minority language. In either case they will be learning the language of most of public life, in a situation where they will be surrounded by that language in education and in much of their own daily life. The other situation is that found in many ex-colonial territories, where the official language is not the language spoken by most people (frequently because there are large numbers of different languages within the country each spoken only by a small minority of the total population). Here, the language of education and government may be taught to almost the whole of the population as a second language, but again it fulfils a definite role in the lives of the learners, who may expect it to be used for many, perhaps all purposes for much of their adult life.

What these two situations share, in contrast with foreign language work, is the fact that it is *necessary* for learners to be efficient in the second language in order to operate fully in society. But of course as learners students will be moving from their mother tongue to a new language, and will therefore have to face problems which will be much greater than those faced by mother tongue users of the official language.

But in fact, when we look closely at second language situations, we see that the matter is much less clear-cut than what has been said above would imply. All societies are to some extent multi-lingual communities, but relations between different languages differ, and many of the difficulties in second language teaching result far more from sociological and political problems than from straightforward problems of students moving from one language to another. Because language is so closely bound up with culture, a decision to learn another language thoroughly may involve repudiating one's own culture, or appearing to do so, and this may have severe social repercussions. We may believe that everyone in Britain should have fluent written and spoken English in order to participate fully in the life of the country, but pupils in schools learning English when their mother tongue is Punjabi or Welsh may be unwilling to identify with the dominant culture to the extent of learning with total commitment. This may be a result of political beliefs (and in many parts of the world language issues provide a focal point for political activity), or it may result from the difficulty of trying to operate in two cultures simultaneously, especially if the dominant one is hostile. However necessary it may appear to the sympathetic outsider for members of minority groups to learn the official or dominant language, there are often compelling reasons on the other side also. What is clear, however, is the complexity of any second language situation. Even if it is true that all mother tongue and foreign language teaching contexts differ, the second language setting, by being between the other two, is never easy to generalise about, and there is no room for dogma.

One striking difference between second language teaching and the other types is that, while most mother tongue and foreign language teaching takes place within the formal school system, much second language provision—particularly for those who have recently moved from one country to another—is for adults. Since this falls outside the normal school system there are often enormously varied approaches taken to this issue. There will be formal teaching in official adult education classes; volunteer teaching in small groups or on a one-to-one basis by teachers who may be untrained, working without payment in their spare time; and classes conducted in factories, through trades unions and through associations of minority group members. Work in this area is uncoordinated, and is particularly vulnerable to financial cutbacks. As a result of the 'fringe' nature of this important activity, teachers are particularly dependent on self-help groups of various kinds, and the specific nature of their work makes it unlikely that publishers will find production of materials a commercial proposition. Consequently, much of the best advice and material is only available through small local groups, and through teachers' associations. The general principles of language teaching, discussed in Chapters Eight and Nine, still apply in these conditions, but they will need adjustment and adaptation. Some help on specific needs in this sphere is offered in the bibliography.

Second language teaching overseas has been, in practice, much more closely related to foreign language teaching in its general assumptions. However, until recently foreign language teaching has not grappled so closely with many of the broad educational implications of language teaching. For many years language teachers in Africa and India, in South East Asia and the South Pacific, have had to consider their work in schools as an adjunct to the process of learning other subjects in English. In many ways their work has been close to that of teachers of mother tongues—but recent developments at tertiary level in traditional foreign language teaching situations have shown that a concern for the content of other subjects is not exclusive to second language work. Nonetheless, courses in English as a second language, designed for largely ex-colonial territories, illustrate well many ways of establishing a full educational context for foreign language work, and repay examination by materials developers from other spheres.

It has frequently been stated that there are major differences between teaching second and foreign languages, and the distinction has been enshrined institutionally. There are often different associations for teachers of EFL (English as a Foreign Language) and ESL (English as a Second Language), and training courses may be organised by different authorities. Indeed, in this book we have perpetuated the distinction by providing separate chapters on the three types of language teaching. However, while we recognise that different social situations produce different kinds of language teaching, we do not consider the differences to be as important as the similarities. As we have tried to show, all language teaching and learning situations differ. The skills and abilities that good teachers bring to bear on language work differ according to context, but they should be based on the same understanding of language and language use. Many of the innovations of the 'Communicative Approach' which have influenced foreign language work in the 1970s have sprung directly or indirectly from work in second language or mother tongue teaching. Mother tongue teachers are showing an increased interest in, for example, the teaching of language for specific purposes, and in the 1960s second language teaching overseas was heavily influenced by developments in foreign language teaching theory. It is probably true that the second language teacher needs to be more sensitive to social and political roles of language than the foreign language teacher—but all teachers need to be aware of this dimension and to build this awareness into their language work. Language teachers need to understand language and to relate this understanding to the social context within which they operate. They also need to know thoroughly the language they are teaching. But the creation of different breeds of language teacher can only lead to professional isolation and suspicion, and this cannot be good for students, who need the benefit of as much expertise and breadth of experience as can be gathered.

This issue is a particularly important one in second language teaching, for this takes place, by definition, in a multilingual context. However professionally separated teachers may be, second language learners use their own language faculties for several different languages. For second language teaching to be at all effective, it must fit—as far as possible—into a setting which includes students' experience of other languages, their past learning styles, the existence or not of mother tongue maintenance classes, the attitudes towards literacy and education, and so on. A second language teacher needs to be able to co-operate with a mother tongue teacher, and with the teacher of English as a mother tongue (into whose class the student may be moving as a successful second language speaker). Better still, the second language teacher and the English teacher may be the same person. But however it works out, in the formal school system always, and as much as possible outside that system, there should be a close relationship between all types of language work, and professional organisation should help, not hinder this process. This is not simply a matter of exchanging methodological hints, though these are important enough, but also of seeing language development as a whole process, as students participate in a multilingual, multicultural society. All countries as the twentieth century draws to an end have become multicultural, and language work is central to the task of ensuring that this development is a step forward, towards greater humanity.

11 Psychology and language teaching

Psychology attempts to study the behaviour of human beings and animals in a detailed, systematic way and to account for this behaviour by finding out what internal forces and what conditions of the mind, the emotions and the body cause them to behave as they do. It has many specialised branches, the psychology of learning being one. The special study of language in psychological terms is usually referred to as 'psycholinguistics', as will have been gathered from Chapter Seven. To anyone interested in language, psychology becomes relevant whenever language is considered not just as a system, but as an aspect of human behaviour, that is, whenever one investigates questions relating to language learning and language use. If we wish to understand what someone has to do, or has done, in learning a language, linguistics will certainly supply some of the information we need, to the extent that it can describe the subject-matter of learning, that is, the structures and systems which constitute the language; but in addition to knowing about the subject-matter, we need to know how and under what conditions people may learn it and apply it, and for much of the information of this sort we have to turn to psychology. Indeed, although psychology cannot yet provide all the information we require, we cannot fail to refer to it in any attempt to understand second and foreign language learning, because while it is to be regarded as highly abnormal for the human individual not to succeed in learning the mother tongue, success in second and foreign languages cannot be taken for granted, and there is evidence that the task of second and foreign language learning can prove quite different for different people, even when external circumstances—the method of instruction, the time spent learning, and so on—appear to be similar. Psychology can at least suggest directions in which to look for the answers to this sort of problem, through its attempts to identify the various factors which seem significant in language learning behaviour and to measure the extent to which people differ in terms of these factors.

The most obvious reason for supposing that the task of second and foreign language learning works out differently for different people is that learners vary vastly in their *achievement* in language learning. Achievement is in fact a measure of how well people perform given tasks, and one can of course only sensibly talk about a person's achievement after adequate opportunity to learn the task in question has been given. A complex task like language learning can be broken down into various levels and types of achievement: to what extent people have mastered a language, and which skills (e.g. reading, writing, speaking) and which functions (e.g. asking for or giving information, persuading, arguing, etc.) they have mastered. There are certain worrying problems with regard to assessing the achievement of language learners, and these are discussed in Chapter Twelve, but the evidence for claiming that differences in achievement exist is overwhelming, whether we are concerned with learners who try to 'acquire' a language without tuition—as in the case of many migrant workers—or with learners who have been given tuition under classroom conditions. It is not uncommon to find learners who can barely string two words together in a language to which they have long been exposed, while some of their fellow learners have achieved a very high competence indeed. No doubt there are sometimes trivial reasons for differences in achievement—for example, that some learners devote more time to learning and practice than do others—and no doubt there are sometimes other reasons which have to do with differences between instructional methods, some of which may be effective, and others not. Nevertheless, there are still grounds for supposing that differences in achievement often stem from factors bound up with the mental make-up and personality of learners.

Aptitude

One inference made by psychologists from the great differences in achievement obtaining between different people in relation to almost any task is that people differ in *aptitude*, which represents the sum of a person's capabilities with regard to particular tasks and skills. With this concept, psychologists have in effect formalised a traditional assumption that people's natural capabilities vary; an assumption expressed in everyday language when we say that someone is 'gifted' or 'specially gifted' or 'has little talent' for something. Whereas it is meaningless to talk of a person's achievement in a task or skill before there has been any opportunity to learn it, aptitude may exist in relation to a task or skill even before it is specifically learnt, and will consequently determine whether learning will be easy or difficult, or, indeed, possible at all. That someone possesses high aptitude for a certain skill, however, does not always mean that he will perform it better than someone else with lower aptitude, since the person with lower aptitude might, for example, work harder at it. When we say, then, that A has higher aptitude for skill X than does B, we are really saying that A should do better in this skill *if* and *only if* everything else remains equal between A and B.

Whether there is a special language learning aptitude, more particularly a foreign-language learning aptitude, and if so, what constituents it has, has not really been resolved, though considerable effort has been invested into tests aimed at measuring it. It has been proposed that factors such as general intelligence, retention (ability to hold things in the memory) and auditory discrimination (ability to hear differences, particularly small ones, between different sounds) are vital ingredients in an individual's language learning aptitude, but the tests so far devised to measure language learning aptitude have not been convincing, which means either that the components of this aptitude have not been properly identified, or have not been properly measured, or that it does not in fact differ crucially as between different individuals, in which case it is not a useful thing to measure. As things stand at present, then, the case for presuming differential aptitude for language learning is far from proven, and, indeed, aptitude as an all-embracing concept may not be very helpful if it disguises the complexity of the enabling and disabling factors involved in any particular individual's attempts at language learning. Nevertheless, the intuitive feeling that people differ markedly in aptitude persists strongly among language teachers and other observers of language learners and, while further research is needed to clarify the matter, the concept perhaps remains useful at an informal level for referring generally to the apparent differential capabilities of language learners.

Transfer

A psychological factor which has emerged as important in attempts to analyse and measure aptitude is *transfer of training*. This is the process by which skills learnt for the performance of a certain task, or skills learnt for application in certain circumstances, are applied in different, but related, tasks or in different, but related, circumstances. If it were not possible to carry over one's training into new situations, learning to do anything would be an exceedingly daunting prospect. Transfer of training, which also includes transfer of prior experience, explains why learning, particularly of new tasks closely related to ones whose performance has been mastered, becomes easier as one proceeds. If one has mastered the violin, the chances are that the learning of another instrument, and especially another stringed instrument, will be very much easier than if one had never learnt the violin, and, at the same time, many general principles of music also. This seems to apply to language learning too; those who have already learnt one foreign language generally find it easier to learn another, and so on. This still begs the wider questions with regard to aptitude, of course, because what one really wants to know is why some people can be successful in learning the first foreign language, and others not, but it is a crucial point in any debate on the usefulness or otherwise of ensuring that everyone has the opportunity of learning at least one foreign language at school. While schools cannot possibly provide any and all languages an individual may need in later life, there is still the argument that the learning of one will provide training and experience which can be transferred if and when needed later on. But transfer of training is also an important consideration in another respect: one usually wants language learners who can cope in the practice-situation of the classroom to be able to transfer their training into the 'real world' where there is no longer a teacher available to help them and their use of language will often entail tangible consequences. It is not in fact immediately obvious that they can do this, particularly if methods of language teaching allow for little practice in the sort of situations in which language is used in the 'real world'—in other words, if language teaching concentrates too much on the purely structural aspects of the language, and too little on the social and cultural contexts in which the language is used and the purposes for which it is used. It would seem then that, at least whenever they can be identified, the sort of situations into which there is to be transfer of training should influence the type of training given.

Attitude

If the thinking behind language teaching, particularly in the school tradition, has tended not to be very explicit about the issue of transfer of training, neither has it always considered as fully as it might the evidence that effectiveness of learning is profoundly influenced by the *attitudes* of the learner towards the task of learning and other things associated with it. It is a commonplace, of course, that someone with a 'negative attitude' towards his work will do less well at it than someone with a 'positive attitude', but what one really needs to know is what promotes various attitudes. This is, admittedly, a notoriously difficult area to study because people are often unwilling to reveal their true, most deep-seated attitudes, and indeed, may often not be consciously aware of what they are. Nevertheless, though the complexities of the relationship between attitudes and language learning are far from understood, research strongly suggests that successful language learners are likely to be those with positive attitudes towards, among other things, the countries and cultures associated with the language being learnt, and unlikely to be those who consciously or unconsciously reject or fear anything foreign, or who feel that their own culture is inherently superior to any other. The founders of the Direct Method appreciated intuitively the connection between positive attitudes and success when they demanded that language teaching should evoke 'sympathy' and 'willing interest', but the more explicit evidence from psychology in recent years has prompted some language teachers and syllabus designers to take the view that it is not sufficient to specify the aims of courses in linguistic terms alone, but that the aims should include 'affective goals', that is, courses should aim to bring about certain overtly specified, positive dispositions towards the cultures and societies in question. Generally, however, it is perhaps not often realised quite what the implications of this whole question are for the organisation of language teaching and the training of language teachers, or how difficult it is to provide conditions under which learners may encounter a foreign culture meaningfully and sympathetically without actually being in it. But it remains a question which cannot be ignored.

Motivation

Attitudes relate to and are included in the wider concept of *motivation*, which is the driving force felt or demonstrated by an individual in carrying out a task. It has been suggested that motivation may be positive or negative, or both at the same time. Negative motivation, not to be confused with lack of motivation, amounts to fear of the consequences of *not* doing what one is supposed to do; fear, for example, of the disapproval, or worse, of parents and teachers. The motivating force then is the desire to avoid unpleasant consequences. Positive motivation, on the other hand, derives from the idea of rewards, which may be concrete, like prizes, or abstract, like the sheer pleasure of achieving something. Unfortunately, as with all other behavioural factors, not enough is yet known about the ingredients, causes and effects of motivation for us to be totally explicit about its relationship with language learning success, though there is general agreement that the higher the degree of motivation, the higher the degree of success will be. One interesting idea that has emerged in recent years is that language learning can be either 'instrumentally motivated' or 'integratively motivated', or both. Instrumental motivation refers to the desire to learn a language in order to achieve some goal not actually connected with the language itself, but for which the language is needed as an 'instrument' in its attainment. Such a goal could be, say, promotion to a job abroad, where promotion is the real goal, and the fact that it is abroad and that the language will be required is incidental. Integrative motivation is held to spring from the desire to master the language for its own sake and to 'integrate' to some extent into the society which speaks it. There is no reason why the same person should not be driven by both types of motivation simultaneously, but in general, it is thought that the most successful language learners are driven by integrative motivation, while those who are instrumentally motivated cease to learn further once they have achieved the minimum competence compatible with attainment of their real goal.

Interlanguage and errors

This last point connects with another interesting idea which has come forward in recent years—the idea of *interlanguage*, which refers to the language of the learner while in the process of learning. At one time, it tended to be thought that learners could be taught foreign languages according to a type of building-block principle, so that at any time in the learning-process, although they could say very little by comparison with a native speaker, what they could say would represent a small chunk of the language in authentic and fully 'correct' form. The illusion that what students said represented what they knew of the language and how they were learning it could however only be maintained while any attempts at spontaneous communication were stifled, and more recent psycholinguistic research, based on the spontaneous utterances of learners, has shown that language learning is not purely incremental, like the building block principle, but progresses in stages, each of which represents a linguistic system. These stages are not stable, however, since the process of learning is a process of change, in this case the change occurring as the learner replaces successive linguistic systems with new ones which correspond more and more with the system of the language being learnt (the 'target language'). At one stage, for example, the learner might have no past tense in the system, then might have a system in which there is the past tense, but with all past-tense verb-forms, including those of irregular verbs, regularised (e.g. 'goed' by analogy with 'snowed', 'sewed', 'called', 'agreed', etc.) and only later a system which begins to show past-tense verb-forms differentiated as between regular and irregular verbs. This is the same sort of process as that undergone by the child learning its mother tongue, except that for the foreign language learner who already has a mother tongue, the mother tongue is an added complication, since the learner, being imbued with its systems and structures, may often impose these upon the target language, thus giving rise to the phenomenon known as *interference*.

Interlanguage, then, may be regarded as the language of the learner while on the journey between mother tongue and target language. Depending on the stage the learner has reached, more or less of the interlanguage will coincide with the systems of the target language, but some of its characteristics may be traced to interference from the mother tongue and some explained in terms of as yet incomplete attempts at acquiring the systems of the language being learnt. Deviations from the forms of this target language constitute *errors*, and where they can be predicted from the stage the interlanguage has reached, they will be *systematic errors*. There may, however, also be deviant elements in the interlanguage which cannot easily be perceived as part of a system, and where these can be taken as the results of guesswork to cover gaps in knowledge, they are to be regarded as *random errors*. Whereas at one time language teachers were encouraged not to create too many opportunities for spontaneous communication, and therefore for errors, the present attitude is to welcome the evidence from the learner's interlanguage and its systematic errors that the process of learning is in motion, and to regard the successive stages in the interlanguage as a yardstick of progress. One further refinement has to be added here, however, and this is that some learners seem to stop learning once they have progressed to a certain level in their interlanguage, and at this level the differences between the forms of the interlanguage and those of the target language, that is to say, the errors, are said to be *fossilised*, since the usual experience is that no amount of corrective treatment will remove them. Perhaps the most plausible explanation of this is that the learners with fossilised errors have attained a level of interlanguage near enough to the system of the target language for all their own communicative needs to be fulfilled, so that there is no drive to progress any further. To come back now to the point about integratively and instrumentally motivated learners, the fossilised error is more likely to be a characteristic of the latter group, since the integratively motivated learner will have a stronger craving for acceptance into the 'target society', which means among other things producing socially valued, and not simply communicatively effective, language forms.

Puberty and language learning

It is open to question whether it is realistic to strive for a very high degree of competence in a foreign language, such that, say, one does not give oneself away as a non-native speaker as soon as one opens one's mouth. There are indeed people who have learnt foreign languages to this level, but debate continues as to whether they are the rare exceptions to the general rule that it cannot be done. The debate focuses mainly on the question of foreign accent, since probably most theorists would now accept that it is possible to learn to understand and manipulate the grammatical structures of a foreign language very competently, but some would maintain that it is not usually possible to eradicate all interference from the mother tongue from the pronunciation of the foreign language once the mother tongue has become stabilised in the individual concerned. This in turn means that the debate essentially hinges upon the effects of *puberty* on language-learning capacity, since prior to puberty there seems to be far less difficulty in acquiring a 'perfect' accent. One view is that the difficulty is caused by physical changes at puberty. It is known that at this time the cerebral cortex of the brain loses the plasticity it has during childhood, and the inference drawn by some is that the motor-programming mechanisms of the brain become 'set', so that attempts to adapt them to the production of new sounds will at best only partially succeed. Another view is that the problem has more to do with psychological changes than with physical changes, since it is at puberty that the individual finally finds a firm identity in a certain culture, whose language is inextricably bound up with the attitudes and values he inherits from the culture. It is not, then, that the learner is physically incapable of speaking foreign languages without an accent after puberty, but that he unconsciously does not wish to, as this would be to give up all signs of attachment to the parent culture and thereby to surrender one's identity. However, certain individuals who have the inner strength not to feel their identity threatened by absorbing a different culture, and perhaps also those who are alienated from the parent culture, will be able to cultivate a 'perfect' accent in the target language. As for children, the claim consistent with this 'psychological view' would be that, not having finally confirmed their cultural identity, they are capable of becoming truly 'bicultural' in a way the adult cannot, and will have no psychological difficulty in acquiring a good foreign accent.

The debate will not be resolved easily, and much remains to be discovered, but it is certainly clear that puberty must be regarded as an important reference-point in respect of language learning capability, and may indeed have even more negative effects for some people than simply militating against a good accent. In fact, it has been suggested that instead of speaking in terms of the mother tongue and foreign languages with reference to children and adults alike, it would be more meaningful to regard all cases of language learning before puberty as cases of first-language acquisition and all cases of language learning after puberty as cases of second or foreign language acquisition. It is around this question of child versus adult language learning capacity that much of the debate on the teaching of foreign languages in the primary school has revolved. Whether it is physical or psychological changes which separate the child from the adult in this matter, it does seem true that there are more problems attendant upon language learning in adulthood than in childhood.

Indeed, it is primarily in relation to adults that the sort of enabling and disabling factors discussed in this chapter are crucial. We may wish to know how and why first language acquisition is so successful and why children seem able to acquire other languages so well, in the context of their abilities as language users, but with adults we are all too often faced with the practical problem of keeping them from failure, and analysis of their problems is therefore vital. There is, however, one great potential advantage the adult should enjoy over the child, and this is the ability to exercise conscious control over the learning process and consciously to bring the skills of analysis to bear on the target language. Because of this, the adult learner has sometimes been claimed to be in principle a more efficient learner than the child. But in order to realise such an advantage, the adult must undertake the venture into unfamiliar territory with a positive disposition, and here the language teacher can help considerably by trying to understand the enabling and disabling, motivating and demotivating factors affecting each learner and by supplying support and encouragement accordingly. It should at least be clear that because of the behavioural dimensions of language learning, and its relationship to the whole personality of the learner, it is insufficient for the language teacher merely to act as a purveyor of the target language.

Memory
In relation to first language acquisition, memory is not usually thought of as a characteristic which distinguishes between people, or even as significant in any way. After all, one can be confident that every normal child will acquire the mother tongue, and if the child seems 'late' in speaking, we do not explain this in terms of a poor memory. Where foreign language learning is concerned, however, memory is generally held to be an important factor. In considering why this should be so, we have to remember the quite often different conditions under which first language acquisition and foreign language learning take place. The conditions surrounding the former allow both constant, repeated exposure to the language and virtually unrestricted opportunities to use it. Typically, the latter takes place in circumstances affording relatively little, even meagre, exposure, and limited opportunities for use. Again, where the former is concerned, language is virtually always used in context, and is used meaningfully to the extent that it contains a 'real message'; with regard to the latter, the language is not always presented to the

117

learner in context, and may be meaningless in the sense that it is not used for 'real communication'. The pressure of time on the foreign language learner and the fact that special strategies have to be adopted to cope with the learning of uncontextualised bits of language which do not readily 'hang together' add up to a burden on the memory, and in this situation, we may begin to perceive some learners as better than others by virtue of possessing a 'better memory'. We may note also that memory seems to become a distinguishing factor once mother-tongue acquisition is transformed, through formal instruction in school, into mother-tongue learning. For example, if children in a mother-tongue class are presented with lists of words to learn on the basis that they are words which the native speaker 'should know', it will immediately emerge that some children can commit them to memory with far greater ease than others.

We have so far used the term 'memory' without offering any definition. In fact, psychologists have identified at least three types, or aspects, of memory of which some knowledge is useful for language teachers. In everyday language, 'memory' usually conveys what psychologists would call *long-term memory*, which is the mechanism or capacity whereby information is held in store over long periods, and can be recalled any time between minutes and years after entry into storage. Long-term memory contrasts with *immediate* or *short-term memory*, the mechanism or capacity for retaining comparatively limited information over short periods. It is known that there is a very definite limit to the amount of information which can be held in this second type of memory; experiments in *recall* have shown that human beings are remarkably consistent in their ability to hold seven, and only seven, chunks of information at one time; attempting to make them hold more units of information causes 'overload' and the loss or rejection of some of the information. Two implications for language teaching emerge straight away: firstly, that the ability of a learner to repeat a series of words or sentences 'on the spot' does not of itself mean that these are entering long-term memory, since the learner could simply be holding them in short-term storage; and secondly, that learners will not hold words and phrases even in short-term memory if these represent too much information at one go. However, here the third type of memory identified by psychologists must be mentioned: *working memory* or *speech processing memory*. This is a complex mechanism called into play in the decoding of speech. The process of decoding requires two important conditions: that the stretch of speech to be decoded be held in immediate memory, and that simultaneously, the knowledge necessary to interpret it—the knowledge that this or that segment represents a noun with a certain meaning, that this or that segment represents a verb with a certain meaning, and so on—be 'called up' from long-term memory and 'applied'. The crucial distinction between short-term memory and working memory is that the former simply retains information over a short period, allowing it to be recalled and repeated, but does not imply any process of interpreting or understanding, whereas the latter must come into play if speech is to be understood. The fact, then, that a learner might repeat a sentence immediately after the teacher does not necessarily mean that working memory is in action at all, which perhaps provides a formal explanation as to why learners putting up an apparently brilliant performance through hours of audio-lingual drilling still may not understand what they have been saying, or be able to say it two hours later. The implications are that if working memory is to be exercised, language must be presented in such a way that it can be interpreted meaningfully; that the task of interpretation, or comprehension, should always be implicit in the general task of learning; and that 'new' language presented must be included in a context which connects with knowlege already present in the learner's long-term memory, whether this context takes the form of known language items or whether it is in some other form, such as a picture or drawing, which makes a connection with the learner's knowledge of the world. Of course, much of this has long been intuitively recognised by teachers, but it seems there is there some formal justification for their intuitions.

In the light of the above, it would seem evident that the task of the language teacher is to try to ensure that what is taught enters the learner's long-term memory. One device used for this purpose over the centuries has been *rote learning* or *rote memorisation*—the committing to memory of long lists of nouns, verbs, verb endings, etc., repeated and recalled mechanically until they are 'known by heart'. This sort of learning is essentially meaningless, in that the material to be learnt is organised into linguistic categories rather than into semantic units. Learning also takes place in advance of its possible application, on the assumption that it will be 'there' when it is required, and that when required and applied, it will become invested with the meaning initially lacking in it. Actually, there are reasons for thinking that this type of learning is not always irrelevant and ineffective, and indeed some recent claims suggest that our capacity to rote-memorise is vastly greater than we might imagine, if only we can overcome the idea that sitting down to memorise huge lists of language items is difficult and boring. Nevertheless, the general implications from psychology would seem to be that if we are to retain information in long-term memory, the information needs to be organised in a way which is meaningful from the outset in the sense that it is *semantically* rather *linguistically* connected; in short, that it contains a 'message'. It also appears to be the case that we are more likely to retain in long-term memory those things which have some impact on us, and interest us. Thus learning a story is likely to be more effective than learning ten sentences; learning how to greet people and say 'goodbye' to them is likely to be more effective than learning a list of words such as: 'hello', 'goodbye', 'handshake', 'to shake someone by the hand'; reading an exciting detective thriller is likely to be more effective than dragging through an account of how the Smith family or Familie Schmidt get up in the morning. Even research on memory, then, seems to suggest that an approach to teaching which emphasises communication and meaningful use of the language is likely to be more effective than one which stresses structure and a dull routine of learning things which may come in useful one day.

Schools of psycholinguistics

It became evident in Chapter Seven that just as there are different schools of thought in linguistics, so there are in psychology also. The longstanding conflict between the empiricist view of human behaviour, a view represented most strongly by the behaviourist psychologists, and the mentalist view represented in modern times by cognitive psychology, is of major concern for language teaching. The empiricist view of human behaviour assumes that behaviour is learnt through experience and through contact with the environment surrounding the individual. Learning is seen not so much as a matter of reflection and understanding as one of developing certain habits through repetition and practice. The learning of one's mother tongue, for example, is seen as a process of developing a whole system of verbal habits. Learning a foreign language is regarded as very problematical, since it means building up a whole new network of verbal habits through often painful repetition and practice, and, inevitably, the new system will clash with the old one, at least initially, causing tremendous interference problems. This conception of language learning, in more or less extreme form, has been very influential in language teaching in the present century, though similar ideas have, less formally, inspired teaching methods over many centuries.

The mentalist view, which conflicts with this empiricist view, is ultimately rooted in the old philosophical conception of man as a reasoning being who has the will to control his environment rather than allowing it to control him. Furthermore, his behaviour is governed by rules, or principles, and is not simply habitual. In this view, a task such as learning a language is not a conditioning process through which a network of verbal habits is developed, but a process of 'cognition', that is, perception, though not necessarily always conscious, of systems of rules, some of which are highly abstract.

Though there is tension between the two views of human conduct outlined here, educators sometimes seem to have been able to combine successfully practices which both views suggest. The Renaissance, for example, was a time of great intellectualism or 'cognitivism', yet Renaissance language teachers used techniques requiring repetition and practice as part of practical training in foreign languages as well as teaching rules. Of course, language teachers should never be inspired more by theories they like or want to 'prove' than by the needs of their students. At the same time, it is impossible to avoid the theoretical debates in psychology if one wishes to see how ideas on the nature of human beings have been translated into practices for teaching them, and if one wishes to acquire a framework in which the behaviour of the language learner can be interpreted systematically. On the issue of empiricism versus mentalism one can only decide for oneself, after more detailed examination of the arguments, which view of human nature one finds more plausible, or more plausible in relation to given aspects of behaviour.

12 Testing: What has been learned?

Perhaps most people familiar with the notion of tests have got to know them from the 'receiving end', probably at school; as a result, it is not necessarily self-evident that tests may be administered for a number of different purposes, and that their construction can be both extremely time-consuming and extremely difficult. Because there is a tendency to use the term 'test' rather loosely, however, we intend here to make a systematic distinction between tests and other forms of evaluation which may be employed by teachers. By a test is meant a measure of knowledge and ability designed to yield information for a specific purpose, and intended to be applied to a specific group of people in such a way that the performance of a particular individual may be compared fairly with that of others in the group. Further, tests are taken under specified conditions and within a specified time-limit. There are a number of important criteria which a test should satisfy if it is to be of value, as we shall see.

Students are often assessed on their performance in exercises as well as tests, but there are significant differences between tests and exercises. Firstly, exercises should above all be designed to help students learn, even if the way they go about learning, as evidenced in their performance in the exercise, is assessed. Tests may indeed teach something, or help students to learn, but if they do in fact fulfil this function, they do it incidentally; their prime purpose is to gauge what has already been learnt or acquired. Secondly, a good exercise for a given group of students should have something in it for everyone, from the best to the weakest, and there need not necessarily be any notion of 'pass' and 'fail' connected with it. Though the information yielded by a test may not in practice be used to pass or fail the people who take it, a test is on the other hand specifically designed to separate people out, and the effect of this may well be that some people cannot complete any of it correctly or even attempt it. It is also worth bearing in mind that, while a bad exercise may not do much good, if important decisions hang on it, a bad test can do a great deal of harm.

Types of test

Though it is convenient to distinguish between 'types of test', it is misleading to think that a test with a different type of content has to be constructed every time one wishes to measure something different. What is far more significant than content in determining what type of test one is employing at any particular time is the use to which the test is being put, that is, the purpose for which one wants the information produced by the test about those taking it. With this very important reservation in mind, we may distinguish between tests administered in connection with language teaching and learning, and indeed in connection with other educational areas, in terms of the following 'types':

1. Achievement or attainment tests

Tests given at the end of a course of study, or at the end of significant stages in it, to determine how well students have coped with the course and how much (or how little) they have learnt, are *achievement* or *attainment* tests. In school, such tests would be the end-of-year examinations or the examinations of the school examining boards which award certificates to successful candidates. There should, of course, be complete correspondence between the content and approach of the syllabus taught and the content and approach of an achievement test. But what does this mean in relation to language learning? While it would plainly be ridiculous if a history syllabus were to specify British social history of the eighteenth century and the test were then to be based on world political history of the nineteenth century, it is not always so easy in language to determine where the boundaries lie between what is legitimate and what illegitimate to test, or what may be considered a fair correspondence between syllabus and test. This is partly because language learning does not usually have a 'content' in the same way as most other subjects, but focuses on the acquisition of skills and abilities which

123

may be applied to a wide range of 'contents'. If, then, essay-writing has been prescribed by a foreign language syllabus and is also to be included in the attainment test, it is arguable that the essay-topics in the test should be different from those treated during the course, to find out whether the requisite skills and abilities have been learnt and can be applied in a novel way, since to repeat the same essay-topics might simply be to invite the 'parroting' of long passages of memorised prose which may not even be understood. Such questions can really only be decided in a principled way, however, in the light of very exact specifications of the goals of the syllabus, which often tend in practice to be phrased quite vaguely, if they are specified at all. Another problem arising with attainment tests is that while, ideally, the test should be based on the syllabus—since it is logical to suppose that the specification of what it is valuable to learn should precede the decision as to what it is appropriate to test—teachers whose students are to be tested at the end of their course in public examinations or other examinations designed without reference to particular teaching-learning situations often tend to base their teaching on the tests, so that the tests themselves in effect determine the syllabus. This problem is known as the *backwash* effect, and perhaps the only way to deal with it is to ensure that the tests causing it at least create beneficial backwash by stimulating useful work rather than sentencing teacher and student alike to irrelevance and drudgery. Finally, it should be mentioned that while attainment tests are in theory only 'backward looking' and would not necessarily claim to say anything about an individual's performance in the future, it is of course in practice the case that they are almost always interpreted predictively by such people as prospective employers, authorities granting places at university, and so on. To what extent this is justifiable may be open to question, but it seems to be a fact of life, especially where there is little other evidence to go on.

2. Proficiency tests

A test which contrasts with the attainment test in having no necessary connection with a syllabus and in marking a beginning rather than an end is the *proficiency* test. Such tests are intended to find out whether those tested are in principle able to carry out given tasks—whether they have the proficiency for them. In this case, then, it is the tasks themselves which will determine the content of the test. Examples of this sort of test are the language tests given to prospective university students from overseas to determine whether they will be able to follow a course of instruction in the language of the country concerned, or those given to overseas doctors to find out whether they can understand and make themselves understood to patients. Of course, it is possible to prepare people for proficiency tests by teaching them to cope specifically with those situations in respect of which proficiency is to be tested, but the tests themselves have no direct interest in such prior preparation, or control over it, and the test-constructor is not obliged to consider the background of those taking the tests beyond the point of establishing in a general way what it is reasonable to expect of them and what may be realistically considered as a minimum acceptable level of proficiency.

3. Aptitude tests

The *aptitude* test is similar to the proficiency test in that it is 'forward looking', but there are several critical differences. Firstly, the proficiency test examines proficiency in doing something which is based on a specific accomplishment—for example, following a university course in which English is the medium of instruction depends upon having accomplished certain skills in English. The aptitude test, on the other hand, does not assume any particular accomplishment, but aims to find out about *potential* or 'natural ability' to do or learn something. Secondly, the proficiency test should evidently and clearly relate in content to the situations for which the people tested are required to be proficient, but the aptitude test cannot do this—it can only be based on the skills or abilities assumed ultimately, and in a general way, to underlie the doing or learning of a specific thing. Thirdly, while people can be prepared for proficiency tests on the basis of a 'syllabus' derived from an analysis of whatever they must be proficient in, it is somewhat nonsensical to think of preparing people for aptitude tests. Practice may improve their performance marginally, but if the theory is correct and what is at issue is really 'natural' potential or ability, then people either have it or they do not. If it is not 'natural' and can be learnt at any time, then the idea of aptitude tests becomes superfluous. Various tests purporting to measure aptitude for learning foreign languages have in the past been developed and tried out fairly widely. They break down the allegedly required aptitude into categories such as 'grammatical sensitivity', auditory discrimination and ability to memorise items of foreign vocabulary. The general consensus of opinion seems to be that while there is some correlation between good performance on such tests and subsequent success in language learning, the reverse does not necessarily hold, so that no-one who does badly in a test of this type should be barred from foreign language learning, even if they should be advised that they might not do very well. As things stand at present, the best predictor of success in foreign language learning is success in learning the first foreign language—but of course this can only apply when it comes to the question of learning a second or subsequent foreign language. (See also the discussion on aptitude in Chapter Eleven.)

4. Diagnostic tests

The final type of test to mention here is the *diagnostic* test. This is both a 'backward looking' and a 'forward looking' test administered at, or between, various stages in a course of learning. It has an interest in the past because it is intended to find out what has and has not already been learnt, but this information is then used to determine what is to be done in the future, particularly with regard to remedial work. It is a test which is useful not only to find out how well students have learnt, but how effective a certain course or type of teaching is, and the tester must always be alert to the possibility that it is not just the learning of the students that needs an overhaul, but the course. If the results are generally bad, then the more the students' results are bunched together, the stronger the latter possibility becomes. The content of a diagnostic test, however, does not necessarily have to be determined in the light of close knowledge of the syllabus followed up to that point. A diagnostic test could be administered, say, right at the beginning of a new course and its content designed to reflect the goals of the course, so that one would then know how students stood in relation to attainment of those goals on the basis of knowledge acquired in the past; but of course a diagnostic test always assumes that in the past there has been opportunity to learn.

Criteria for effective tests

We said earlier that there were certain criteria which a test should satisfy if it is to be of value. This is a statement of the ideal, since there is, unfortunately, no escaping the fact that it is not realistic to expect tests constructed under pressure of time by teachers with no highly specialised knowledge of testing to measure up to these criteria in every respect. Furthermore, as it is a time-consuming operation involving statistical procedures actually to prove that tests satisfy all the requirements, this sort of hard proof can hardly be called for every time a teacher sets a class a test or an end-of-year examination. Our remarks here will then apply more particularly to test batteries intended to be taken by large groups of people, possibly over many years, and on which crucial decisions are based—such as language tests for overseas university students and public examinations on the basis of which university places are awarded and offers of employment made. However, there are still some important criteria against which even the most humble test can be checked, and we will suggest which these criteria are later on.

We have already, in effect, stated one of the very first requirements of a test by saying that tests are designed to separate people out and to allow comparison of the performance of a particular individual with that of others in the same group—to put this more technically now, a test must *discriminate,* which means that it must allow for a range of different performances. At least, it must do this in principle, even if by some strange chance performances vary very little on a given occasion on which the test is used. Tests are designed for *populations*, which can be defined in any way that is relevant—for example, all prospective overseas university students to whom English is a foreign language, all 16 year-olds about to leave school, all 11 year-olds about to proceed to the secondary school, and so on. If one now wishes to measure a particular attribute in relation to this population—say, knowledge of a foreign language or mathematical ability—then one must pitch the test at a level which corresponds to reasonable expectations about the distribution of the attribute in this population. The test should not be too easy for this population, or everyone will do well and the potentially better candidates and 'high-flyers' will have no opportunity to make themselves apparent, and it should not be too difficult, or it will not only work to the detriment of weaker candidates who may in fact be capable of a tolerable performance if tested fairly, but will generally yield more information about what people cannot do rather than what they can. Again, a test cannot be expected to discriminate in a meaningful way if administered to a population for which it was not designed—a test designed for 11 year-olds may entirely lose its discriminatory value if administered to 15 year-olds, a test designed for learners of a foreign language may not discriminate if administered to native-speakers, and so on. Classroom teachers dealing with small populations they know intimately—their own classes—will usually have good intuitive appreciation of the distribution of any particular attribute in these populations, and their intuitions should be able to help them pitch the test in such a way that it will discriminate between good, average and weak performances in terms of these populations. Where tests are being constructed for large populations, however, there are special procedures to be used for determining how well a test discriminates, and these procedures are applied using *samples* of the population before the test is considered ready to employ in earnest. Of course, where a test is used for the purpose of 'passing' and 'failing' candidates, it is up to the tester or agency employing the test to fix the pass-mark. In large populations, one would expect a distribution of performances on any particular attribute such that there are few really 'high-flyers', few candidates who can do next to nothing, and a big bunch of candidates in the middle between just below average to just above average—but where one places the pass-mark will still depend on the purposes of the test. If it is intended to select a few people for special scholarships, for example, then obviously 'average' must fail and the pass-mark will be high. If it is to award school-leaving certificates, which usually indicate standards of performance anyway, then 'average' will usually pass, and so on. But the essential point is that tests, as instruments designed to produce information about how individuals in a population compare with other individuals in that population in terms of a given attribute, are useless if they do not discriminate.

Another criterion which tests should satisfy is that of *reliability*. This essentially means that a test should be so constructed that performances on it are not random but are actually procured in a systematic way through the interaction of the test with the knowledge and ability of the individuals tested; so that, if the test were repeated, the results obtained should still place candidates in the same rank order. The sort of thing likely to make a test unreliable would be, say, ambiguous phrasing of questions, such that the same individual sees different meanings in them on different days. Or again, unreliability could, and all too often does, lie in the marking procedures, which may be underspecified or leave too much scope for the subjective judgments of different markers; and it is of course important to bear in mind that the marking, or *scoring* of a test, as it is usually called, is an integral part of the test and needs to be considered from the very beginning. Proving reliability, however, is hardly realistic for anyone not constructing tests to be used on a large scale or for the purpose of making crucial decisions affecting people's lives, where of course, reliability should be beyond question. There are several procedures for proving reliability which can be used with samples of the population to be tested. The commonest are the test-retest procedure, where the same test is administered again to the same subjects after an interval just long enough for them to forget the details, but not long enough for them to change in any significant way in relation to each other; and the other is the 'split-halves' procedure, where two parallel versions of a test are made up from the same pool of material and each 'half' administered to the same subjects on different occasions. Both procedures should show the scores of each individual to be in the same rank-order in both occasions. Where procedures such as these are impracticable, the only recourse is to examine a test very carefully from the viewpoint of everything which might make it unreliable and to eliminate as many possible causes of unreliability as one can.

The final criterion a test should measure up to is *validity*, which may be sub-divided into validity of different sorts. The first thing we would normally expect a test to show is *face validity*, Does a test look, in quite general terms, as though it tests what it claims to test? In language, a test would seem to lack face validity if, say, it included a translation passage where translation was of relevance neither in the syllabus nor, in the case of a proficiency test, in the situations in which the language was subsequently to be used. If a test does not have face validity, then there is an obligation on the test constructor to show that despite this lack the test does nevertheless test what it is supposed to test. Face validity, then, is the first and simplest point in the check-list against which a test is to be assessed. A rather more detailed examination of the test will then be required to determine whether it has *content validity*. If it is an attainment test, does it really reflect the syllabus? Has anything crept in anywhere which students could not in fact be required to know? If it is a proficiency test, does it in fact relate to the task for which proficiency is required? Does it demand anything that is not required, or omit anything that is required? If a test appears to have content validity, then it should also be expected to show *concurrent validity*. This means that it should produce results which are in line with other tests or evaluations in respect of any particular individual taking it. If the results of a test are strongly at variance with other evaluations, then something would seem to be wrong somewhere, and the test must come under suspicion. Of course, it may be that the other measures are wrong, but one needs to be certain. Another type of validity which a test may or may not satisfy is *predictive validity*. This is quite an important concept with regard to major tests on which serious decisions are based. What this validity amounts to is that the later performance of the people who have taken such tests should tend to confirm that the tests did at the time assess them fairly. Do, say, overseas university students assumed to have no problems with the language of instruction because of a good performance on a language proficiency test in fact turn out to have no problems? Or were the results of the test, in retrospect, misleading? Obviously, establishing the predictive validity of tests is a long-term matter, and it may not be easy to decide what criteria of later success or failure should be used to measure it. Measurement also involves quite complex statistical procedures. But those who produce tests known to be used for predictive purposes associated with important decisions should feel an obligation to demonstrate the validity of their tests in this respect.

Another type of validity which we must mention is *construct validity*. In the field of language testing this is usually taken to mean that tests should be constructed in such a way as to reflect current thinking on the aims of language teaching and the nature of language learning, but obviously, as views on language teaching and language learning change, so do ideas about what constitutes construct validity. It is probably not far wrong to assert that the major debates in testing are in essence debates on construct validity, triggered by changes or conflicts of view about language teaching matters generally. It has been claimed, and it seems reasonably, that the history of language testing in this century falls into three stages. The first, 'pre-scientific' stage was one in which concepts such as reliability and validity were not even considered, and tests were mainly of the essay and translation type. The second stage came in with structural linguistics, which took an 'atomistic' view of language, insisting that language facility could be broken down into different skills which had to be be taught and tested separately; and as a consequence the *discrete-point* language test, which measured such things as knowledge of vocabulary, knowledge of grammar and knowlege of phonology and phonetics separately, became the norm, at least for professional testers. At the same time, foreign language tests were influenced by, and sometimes based entirely on, contrastive analysis. It was also at this stage that testing took on a new 'rigour' with the adoption of statistical procedures and mathematical concepts. The third stage, the current stage, has come about with the idea of communicative competence, which looks upon language as an integration of skills, abilities and knowledge, not all of which are strictly linguistic, working together for communicative effect, and the trend is now away from the discrete-point test and towards the *integrative* or *global* language test. These stages in testing reflect, then, the major phases in foreign language teaching this century — grammar-translation, audiolingualism, communicative language teaching—and it will be evident that language testing cannot be independent of language teaching, and that the same underlying views will affect the way both are conducted.

Those now in favour of integrative tests make much of techniques such as dictation, which they see as a measure of total language proficiency—success in it requires a 'predictive' ability which only someone who really knows the system of a language, and knows how people behave in that language, can possess. For the same reason, there is also a considerable interest in *cloze* tests, whereby words — typically every fifth—are deleted from a text and the candidates tested then have to supply these missing items by reference to the surrounding context. Claims for the efficiency and economy of such tests have been made on the basis that much more complicated test-batteries provide no more information and are no more reliable. There is also much interest in the idea of *criterion-referenced* tests, as opposed to the more traditional norm-referenced tests, which set those tested communicative tasks of the sort found in 'real life' and assess the total—not just strictly linguistic—performance on these tasks. Such developments are of course in line with current thinking, and many would not now accept the construct validity of tests which separate linguistic skills or separate the use of language from 'real' communicative situations. However, in spite of the general agreement on the value of communicative teaching, there still remains the argument that inasmuch as linguistic skills are part of communicative skills, and inasmuch as one can focus attention on linguistic skills and single them out for special treatment in teaching, one can also single them out for treatment in testing where this is appropriate—as it very often is, say, with diagnostic tests. Because communication requires a working together of linguistic and other skills, this does not in fact mean that they cannot be separated out. In the end, the teaching and learning of language, and indeed of communication, depends both upon analysis and synthesis. Where analysis is appropriate, it may still justify the discrete-point test, but deciding where analysis, and where synthesis, is appropriate is a matter of specifics and not of generality. By this token, construct validity can only be determined in the light of particular objectives and not of general trends.

Informal classroom tests

There are certain procedures of checking the reliability of tests which the classroom teacher could not normally be expected to apply when putting together a routine test, and if no really significant decisions depend upon the outcome, this may not really matter as it would with a more major test. But, as we said earlier, there are still some important criteria against which even the most humble tests could be checked, without elaborate statistical procedures. In the light of one's knowledge of a particular group or class, will the test discriminate? Does it have face validity, and if not, why not? Does it have content validity (or is one being unfair)? Does it turn out to have concurrent validity, and if not, could it be that the test was at fault? Even checking tests at this sort of everyday level, but checking them over carefully, could conceivably ensure that a little more justice is done a little more often.

In this chapter we have discussed testing largely from the point of view of foreign language testing. This is because—since foreign language teaching almost always leads to some form of certification —there is a great deal of experience to call upon in this field, and the theoretical difficulties can be discussed with maximum clarity. In the fields of second and—particularly—mother tongue teaching, social influences make the whole discussion of testing much more difficult to clarify. Indeed, many people would argue that there is something illogical about *testing* the mother tongue usage of normal speakers. On the other hand there are many aspects, of written work particularly, regarding which society demands some indication of comparative abilities from schools. What is clear is that, making due adaptation for the different social roles of different kinds of language teaching, the principles outlined in this chapter have relevance to any discussion of language testing, and they need to be understood by all teachers. Testing is used for research purposes, and as an instrument of social selection for universities, training and employment. Even teachers who have no wish to use such instruments themselves need to understand what examiners and researchers are doing, if only for self-protection.

13 Technology for language teaching

From the earliest times, teachers have striven for ways of improving their teaching and making learning easier and more certain, and they have looked to technology for assistance. When we speak of technology in language teaching and learning, however, we can mean one or both of two rather different but connected sources which provide assistance, and influence the way in which teaching and learning are organised.

First, there have been many technological innovations in the world at large, such as the printed book, the tape recorder and the slide-projector, which, though not directly inspired by the needs of the language teacher and learner, are used for teaching and learning purposes. In this sense, then, the products of 'external' technology have been incorporated into language teaching and learning, and as a result of the wide-ranging technological developments of the present century in particular, teachers today have available to them a great range of technical resources to help them in their teaching, while learners have never before had such opportunities as are offered through these resources to find the type of assistance which suits them best.

However, in order to make appropriate use of the products of technology in general and to bring improvements in other ways, teaching and learning have generated round themselves their own technology, known as educational technology, and this technology has become more complex as the variety and sophistication of technical resources have increased. To see why there is a need for a specialised educational technology separate from other technologies, we have to appreciate that in essence 'technology' refers not to devices and gadgets, even though in everyday speech we tend to use the term in this meaning, but to a set of systematic procedures for carrying out practical tasks and solving practical problems efficiently. The word 'systematic' is important, because practical problems are not always solved in a systematic way. Sometimes solutions emerge through trial-and-error or are based on intuition and common-sense. Indeed sometimes they have to be found by intuition because the principles involved in a problem and its solution are not explicitly understood. A technology, however, can be set up wherever there is some relevant scientific knowledge to draw on, and it then proceeds in accordance with the principles of the scientific system from which that knowledge derives, on the assumption that this type of approach is likely to lead to success more quickly and consistently than any other. There can in theory be as many technologies as there are practical tasks to perform and problems to solve, though we usually set up or identify technologies only round more complex tasks and problems, in fields in which we expect advances in scientific knowledge to contribute to the refinement of the technology.

Now, it has to be remembered that when we use a piece of technical equipment in the language classroom, we are usually engaged in the exploitation of that equipment for purposes which may never have occurred to its inventor. If we use a tape recorder, for example, we are only incidentally involved in the technology of sound recording and reproduction in connection with which it was developed, our central concern being to exploit it for the benefit of teaching and learning. This process of exploitation can, then, be regarded in itself as a specialised technology, firstly because it focuses on attempts to solve the special practical problems of teaching and learning, secondly because the decisions and procedures involved are of considerable complexity, and thirdly because there is at least some systematic, even if not truly scientific, knowledge to guide these decisions and procedures. In the case of language teaching and learning, this systematic knowledge derives from linguistics as well as psychology and general theories of education. So technology in language teaching and learning covers both technology in the general sense and its products such as tape recorders, film-projectors and television sets, and technology in the more specialised sense of educational technology.

The subject of educational technology is complicated by disagreements over its scope and potential. At one extreme, some people consider it as being limited more or less to the science or art of using technical aids and resources for educational purposes. At the other, there are those who claim that the whole of education can be regarded as a technology and that, ultimately, when we have enough relevant knowledge, it will be possible to systematise teaching and learning in almost every detail. In this latter view, technical aids and resources are useful and are to be employed whenever appropriate, but are not absolutely central to educational technology: they are to be seen as only one part of a complete system whose other parts include syllabuses, methods, materials, teachers and learners.

Another debate revolves around the status of the systematic and scientific knowledge on which educational technology draws. It is quite true that from psychology and linguistics, for example, we can derive principles to be applied and followed in organising language teaching and learning, but not only do theories in psychology and linguistics tend to change more often and more radically than those in fields such as chemistry and physics—they also tend to overlap and conflict with each other. Therefore, even if one does accept that educational technology can be regarded as a technology in the same way as any other, one still has to admit that when and while there are conflicting theories in psychology and linguistics as well as about the purposes of education, there can at one and the same time be several technologies operating in accordance with rather different principles, but all grouped together within the concept 'educational technology'. There are of course general trends which contribute to the maintenance of unity—for example the trend towards communicative teaching and away from grammar-based teaching, but these changes in trend also entail changes in educational technology—in the case in point the organisation and techniques appropriate to communicative teaching being different from those appropriate for grammar-based teaching. Without pursuing the theoretical problems of educational technology in detail here, we shall give one or two examples of ways in which technology in the more abstract sense of 'teaching and learning procedures' has changed in response to shifts in theory. We shall do this, however, by approaching the question of technology through discussion of some of the aids and resources made available through technological developments in the general sense. After all, while it may be true that educational technology as an attempt to systematise teaching and learning is not always crucially dependent on the existence of technical devices and gadgets, it is only since the technological developments of the last few decades began to open up quite dramatic new possibilities for improving teaching and creating better conditions of learning, thereby also introducing new organisational complexities, that educational technology has gained explicit recognition.

Hardware and software

The technical resources used to assist teaching and learning are by convention identified either as *hardware* or *software*. The former category covers all devices, gadgets and machines such as record players, tape and cassette recorders, slide and film projectors and video recorders. The latter category includes all 'consumable', 'replaceable' and 'modifiable' items such as gramophone records, tapes, cassettes, slides, film and video cassettes. Textbooks, exercise books, disposable materials for writing on and, indeed, teaching and learning materials in general, are also regarded as software. Now it is evident that some types of software can be used without the need for any special hardware, but most hardware is a vehicle for software. We know that the blackboard, for example, or something similar to it, is a piece of hardware dating from many centuries ago, and we can say that it is still one of the most valuable pieces around. But its value is not intrinsic—it is valuable only in that it allows the use of chalk to write and draw. In the same way, a projector has a value while there are films to show with it; without films it is useless. What follows from this is that the usefulness of any piece of hardware will depend on the usefulness of the software, or, more precisely, the uses to which the software can be put.

As well as being divided into hardware and software, technical aids and resources are also categorised as between *audio* and *visual* aids, the former serving to reproduce or convey sound and the latter to show pictures or other visual displays. Thus a tape recorder is an audio aid and a slide projector a visual aid. Though all aids of this sort are referred to collectively as audio-visual aids, true audio-visual aids are hybrids which combine sound with pictures or other visuals —television and films are an example.

Visual aids have a much longer history than audio aids. We have already referred to the blackboard, which seems to have made its appearance in about the third century AD. Charts depicting the structure of the target language were also in use very early on, and coloured pictures were in common use in the latter half of the nineteenth century. Sometimes pictures are used simply to illustrate texts in a general way, to add interest and heighten the learner's curiosity about the written text. Sometimes they are used as memory-clues, to help the learner call to mind the vocabulary and structures associated with a certain situation. Sometimes they are used expressly to convey meaning, especially where use of the students' mother tongue is either proscribed, as in the 'purer' versions of the Direct Method, or not practicable. However, pictures of this last type can often be misleading, especially where interpretation is open to cultural variation, and one has to be careful with them. In general, though, pictures can still serve as very useful aids in language teaching and learning without necessitating complicated technology—for example, a comic-strip series of pictures can stimulate learners into constructing a narrative, or, with words removed from the 'thought' and 'speech' bubbles, can prompt work on spoken dialogue round various situations. The coming of photography widened the application of pictures. Photographs could now be used to give realistic impressions of what foreign countries were like, thus increasing interest in foreign cultures, as well as to add authenticity to texts and narrations. Colour photography, slides, moving pictures and, of course, television have added considerably to the realism which it is possible to conjure up in the classroom. The more sophisticated types of visual software have a special application in communicative teaching since, inasmuch as one is concerned to prepare learners to communicate in 'real-life' situations, the more one can do in the practice situation of the classroom to conjure up the feeling of such situations and engender familiarity with them, the better the learners will be prepared to venture into the outside world and use their new language. But again, the right visual aid has to be chosen for the right purpose. In the early stages, and especially when teaching structures, the blackboard and simpler aids will often be very adequate. When students can begin to construct dialogue, an aid such as the ciné-loop projector, which shows ten to fifteen minute cartoon-type silent films round and round in a continuous circuit might be just the thing to stimulate dialogue production. To maintain interest and broaden vocabulary, television programmes either of restricted scope or specially made for language learning might be used, and at a very advanced stage, when students can discuss issues and reconstruct situations and narrative with some sophistication, perhaps authentic television programmes made for native speaker audiences.

Speech

Though it is difficult to isolate the importance of particular technological developments for language teaching, perhaps the most significant since the printed book has been the advent of speech recording and reproduction. Before this was possible, learning for oral communication, or practising the spoken language in anything but a most rudimentary way, was very difficult indeed without the help of a native speaker or a teacher with very high competence in the spoken language. That there was a shortage of non-native teachers with adequate competence in the spoken language became evident when attempts were made to popularise the Direct Method in schools, at least in Britain. Many teachers just could not 'model' the language adequately for their students. Sound-recording made authentic models available, however, even if at a remove, and teachers whose competence in the oral language was not very high, but who could nevertheless organise their students to learn, could now present the target language in oral form via recordings and begin to cultivate at least some oral competence in their students. Furthermore, sound-recording also opened a whole new dimension to those who wished or needed to study a language on their own, and learning a language from disc or tape at home remains very popular.

But while being able to record the speech of native speakers was in itself an immeasurably significant breakthrough, especially for advanced learners and scholars, just hearing the target language spoken by native speakers is not usually in itself adequate for learning. What most teachers and learners would regard as critical is the way that the recorded utterances are organised; in short, how they are structured as materials. It is at this point that educational technology must meet the 'external' technology of speech-recording and exploit it for its own purposes, just as it exploits the availability of print for written materials. It just so happened that due to a very neat historical accident, speech-recording was reaching the point at which it could be exploited conveniently and on a large scale when a very forceful movement in language teaching, the movement behind the Audio-Lingual Method, could find an almost indispensable use for it. It is a tenet of the Audio-Lingual Method that what it identifies as the 'four skills' of language learning are to be learnt in the order:

Listening (or understanding of the spoken word), Speaking, Reading (or understanding of the written word) and Writing. It is also axiomatic to cultivate a good accent and pronunciation. The practical consequence, then, is that a great deal of work has to be done on the oral side with this method, but it was realised that if most, or indeed all of this oral work could be directed through recordings made by native-speakers, the method would not be confined to those classrooms in which the teachers possessed relatively exceptional competence in the spoken language. At the same time, the exercises accompanying this method, at least in 'pure' form, require much repetition and oral manipulation of the language, which can be extremely fatiguing for the teacher directing the class, so having all the teaching materials on tape or disc was seen as a great advantage. The Audio-Lingual Method, then, though not in essence dependent as a method on speech-recording, did much to spread the use of recordings in language teaching. Furthermore, it inspired the development of a very thorough and intricate technology for the exploitation of speech-recording in order to turn the recorded utterances of native speakers into language teaching materials. However, the popularity of the method was in many quarters short-lived. It did not catch on in schools on the scale at first expected, not least because many students found it boring. Also, the theoretical underpinnings of the whole approach to language teaching embodied in the Audio-Lingual Method came under fierce attack from linguists, and for many the method lost credibility. The interesting point about this is that as a consequence, the whole technology developed to turn speech-recordings into materials for the Audio-Lingual Method, and to organise teaching around these materials also lost credibility.

Educational technology—in this case exemplified in the work of producing Audio-Lingual materials—cannot, then, be independent of teaching and learning theory. It is informed by this theory, and has to respond to it. Today, though there is in fact still some application for materials of the Audio-Lingual type, the major theoretical force is in favour of communicative teaching, and audio materials, as well as other materials, reflect this new approach, which in turn demands a new and rather different technology.

The language laboratory
For many people, the piece of audio hardware most readily associated with language teaching is the language laboratory. The

name is perhaps not altogether apt. The language laboratory in its most common current form is a collection of tape or cassette recorders, each one usually located in a booth-type arrangement with sound-deadening side-panels to isolate it from the others. Learners sit one to a booth and wear earphones in order to listen to the recorded material playing on their tape or cassette machine. In all but the simplest laboratories, each learner also has a microphone, usually combined in a headset with the earphones, with which to record his own voice onto the cassette or tape wherever this is necessary in carrying out exercises. The tape machines are specially adapted so that the learners' recordings cannot erase or spoil any exercise material already recorded on the tape. The idea of having the learners record is twofold: first, learners should be able to compare their own utterances from the point of view of pronunciation and correctness with the utterances of the native speakers recorded on their tapes. However, learners often cannot hear or detect their own mistakes, particularly in the early stages. So, second, the language laboratory is arranged in such a way that a teacher, sitting at a control-panel, can listen in on each learner's work and get learners to replay the work they have been doing and have recorded on their tapes. The teacher can then correct, help and encourage as necessary. The more sophisticated laboratories are very flexible, can be used for anything from just listening to authentic speech through to working on interpreting exercises, and allow both for individual and group work. The laboratory, like the use of speech recordings, was largely popularised through the Audio-Lingual Method, indeed was identified with this method by many, so that when the method lost credibility, so too did the language laboratory. However, though it is perhaps no longer regarded as being quite so central to language teaching as it once was, it has tended to regain popularity now that new and more communicative types of audio materials are being produced.

Aids to individualisation

In Chapter Eight we mentioned the current trend towards individualisation in language learning, a trend based on the view that in the past too much attention has been focused on teaching, and that in future more should be focused on learning, as well as on the view that each learner should be clearly recognised as an individual, with individual aims, motivations, abilities and learning strategies. Operating individualisation on a large scale, with the emphasis on the effectiveness of teaching and learning just as much as on efficiency, is of course not easy, but technical aids can do much to facilitate it.

It is normally considered that there are four areas to take into account in offering individualised learning programmes: objectives; pace of learning; methods; materials. A thoroughgoing attempt at individualisation, then, would require giving a choice in all these areas, or, better still, allowing learners to put together their own programmes, with appropriate advice from the teacher, in relation to all these factors. Interestingly, though few institutions will be able to afford such an investment in the immediate future, the computer would probably represent in principle the most useful piece of hardware one could have available for this type of 'all-out' individualisation, since it can not only store a vast amount of teaching material and present it via different channels in written, visual and oral form, but it can also be programmed to monitor the progress of learners through tests and exercises and to prescribe remedial work, all on an individual basis, and far more tirelessly than a human teacher. If it had sufficient terminals for all the learners in a particular group, it could subsume all the functions of a language laboratory and expand them into a 'multi media laboratory' designed to meet the requirements of each individual learner. Indeed, the computer is already in limited use for language teaching purposes, and has shown great promise, so that these remarks are not in any way speculative, but based on some experience. Even if we assume that many institutions could afford a computer, however, the major problem to be faced would be the programming, since this is not only extremely time consuming, but outside the competence of most language teachers. But this again is a problem which is receiving attention, since attempts are at this moment being made to develop a simplified computer language—EXTOL—which even the least numerate language teacher can acquire and use for programming.

In spite of the signs that the computer is beginning to have a useful application in language teaching, we probably have to accept that it is in general terms a device of the twenty-first century rather than of the twentieth where most language teachers and learners are concerned. However, all the more usual technical aids can assist individualisation, subject only to the requirement that the teacher does not feel the need—or, indeed, the neurotic anxiety—to keep everyone in a certain group to the same activities at the same time. The language laboratory, for example, becomes infinitely more useful once the teacher begins to consider how learners can profitably spend time in it on their own. It can help immediately with regard to pace of learning if it is available outside class hours on a *self access* basis, since those who need extra practice, or who want to forge ahead with their work, can then gain entry to it as required. It can also be employed to diversify methods. For example, the same grammatical point can be taught in a wide variety of ways. The conditional in English might be taught as a matter of tense and morphology, or within the context of dialogues in which people talk about what they *would* do, given certain conditions. After a general presentation to the class, the teacher could send off to the laboratory those who preferred to learn inductively, through example, imitation and practice, to listen to dialogues, and could work further with those who felt they needed 'explicit' teaching. Again, the laboratory can be used to diversify materials. All that is required for such diversification is a bank of pre-recorded tapes and abandonment of the assumption that a laboratory session begins with the transfer of a master-recording from the teacher's control panel, or console, which is usually a time-wasting procedure in any case. Again, the *reading laboratory* is a most useful device for allowing individual pacing. All this boils down to is a large box of cards, each containing a reading passage with comprehension questions at the end, arranged in accordance with some grading system, a 'key' or some other means of giving feedback after the comprehension questions have been done, and some way of keeping a record of each individual's progress. There is no reason, either, why resources such as video tapes should not be used for diversification, if some learners in a group can watch television in one part of the room while others are reading or are in the language laboratory. The teacher should not 'hoard' equipment and resources, or be afraid to instruct learners how to operate machines (so long as this is permitted by the relevant education authorities). If individualisation is to be practised at all, teachers should regard themselves as a resource which needs distributing among the learners, giving them individual assistance and feedback as required. To step from behind the teacher's desk is not to give up teaching, but possibly to do it more effectively.

We said in Chapter Eight that the practicability of individualisation does not depend entirely on the availability of technical aids, even though they can assist it greatly. However, whether one has the most sophisticated aids, or only 'paper resources', one near-essential is the *learning packet*. This consists of one unit of work which may be put together according to various criteria: it may deal with a structural point, it may be intended to provide reading practice or a problem-solving exercise, to be done by one learner, or by a pair, or by a group. The ideal would be to build up a whole bank of learning packets graded according to difficulty, diversified according to content and designed for use by a varied number of people. The packets could, of course, contain tapes or videotapes where such resources were available, but where not, they could include written and visual materials ranging from summaries of grammar to magazine articles. They could also include references to standard textbooks, of which there should be a range—indeed, where textbooks are concerned, it is probably better, in the individualised classroom, to have available a few copies of as many different texts as possible, than to spend all one's available finance on one set of the same text. Getting such a system organised obviously takes time and energy, and should be thought of as a long term, ongoing operation. It cannot be done overnight.

Radio and television
A brief mention should be made here of radio and television. In Britain, both these media are responsible, through their language courses for the general public, for some fine work in educational technology. They bring syllabuses, materials, teaching techniques and an exploitation of the possibilities of the media together very successfully, so much so that although most of the language courses are designed for study without a teacher, teachers often record the programmes and use them with their students.

Technology will always have a place in language teaching and learning, but it will never remain static. The innovations of 'external' technology will continue to add potential new resources for language teaching, and educational technology will continue to exploit them in response to the needs of language teachers and learners and in the light of contemporary thinking on teaching and learning.

Nevertheless, there are a number of concerns which will constantly engage the attention of specialists in educational technology.

Efficiency will be one—how to effect teaching and organise learning most economically in terms of time, effort and financial expenditure. This means being clear about the goals to be attained and finding the best possible ordering and structuring of the teaching and learning materials. Effectiveness will be another—how to ensure that as a result of teaching, learning actually takes place. This means matching the teaching to the learners, discovering the most appropriate media for the presentation of materials, setting the learners objectives they can realistically be expected to achieve, and finding ways of maintaining, or better still, increasing motivation. It also entails obtaining feedback—information on the effects of this or that procedure or the use of this or that technical aid, so that modifications can be made. Rational planning of resources will be another concern. Does a school really need a language laboratory, for example, when a number of portable cassette recorders would serve just as well for the purposes it has in mind? Again, whatever resources are available in theory, they are not always all available in practice, which means keeping an open mind with regard to 'alternative technologies'. By the same token, there can be no really fixed relationship between technical resources and teaching and learning. In language teaching and learning just as in any other educational field, technology essentially means getting what current knowledge on all aspects of teaching and learning would indicate to be the best out of what one has at one's disposal. It cannot be denied, however, that the greater the range of technical resources available in any given situation, the greater the chances of satisfying the purposes and needs of teachers and learners, and the fewer the constraints on course-planning. All other things being equal, today's technology can give today's language learner better chances of success than any language learners of the past.

14 Designing a language course

It may be felt that neither course design, nor teacher training (the subject of Chapter Fifteen), are really suitable for an introductory book on language teaching. There are two reasons, however, why we feel that it is important to include a brief discussion of both of them. One is that right from the start of their careers all teachers have to experience training and to teach to a particular course organisation, so they need some understanding of the principles they are being exposed to. The other is that many teachers increasingly find that they are expected to design courses and to help train other teachers quite early in their careers.

Furthermore, although the connection may not immediately be apparent, we feel that these two topics are closely related. The training of teachers should not be something which happens once and for all at the beginning of their careers, but should be a continuing process of education. The development of effective teaching courses is also a continuing process, and—after the period of initial training—teacher development and course improvement begin to become one and the same thing. Let us begin, however, by discussing the issues separately before turning to the ways in which they can be brought together.

Principles of course design
As we have argued in Chapters Eight and Nine, some sort of organising pattern is essential for any teacher, but the exact nature of that organisation will depend on the assumptions made—usually implicitly by the institution or a higher body like a Ministry of Education—about the nature of language learning and the appropri-

ate aims of education. However, there are some general points worth making which apply to all syllabuses.

1 A syllabus leads towards a goal. The justification for a government enforcing compulsory education, or for students or their parents paying for schooling, is that experience of organised education helps learning to develop more effectively than through disorganised experience. A syllabus must therefore help a learner to achieve certain goals.

2 A syllabus must have a starting point (which must be where the learners actually are) as well as an end point, so it implies movement from one position to another.

3 A syllabus is a practical instrument, and it is judged by its success or failure. It is no good having an ideal syllabus which is unacceptable to either teachers or students, so any syllabus must fit in with the realities of people, organisations, teaching materials, and so on.

4 Since we usually teach classes, a syllabus involves generalisations about learners. In practice, teaching cannot be related to each separate, individual student. (In fact, as language is a social activity this is not really a disadvantage.)

5 A syllabus can only specify what is to be offered to the student; it cannot predict exactly how the student will learn what is offered. This is partly because students may tend to learn in different ways, but also because ways of learning depend heavily on complex patterns of motivation which will vary from time to time and situation to situation. The methodology of the teacher will be able to respond sensitively to these differences, but no syllabus can be flexible enough to predict all such possible variations.

6 A syllabus is thus a statement of the organisation of the material to be taught. This organisation will reflect general principles, and the main justification for making such a statement is so that the general principles and the specific organisation can be discussed and improved upon, as a result of changing ideas in language study and education. These changing ideas will come partly from research, but far more from the experience of teachers using the syllabus and materials deriving from it. Their experience will of course reflect changing social needs for language teaching.

A syllabus of the kind defined above will underly any teaching programme and any set of learning materials. However, it may not be made explicit, and it may therefore be very difficult to describe and to criticise. If, however, we really believe in improving our teaching, it is necessary for us to make such underlying principles explicit so that they can be understood, criticised and improved. To refuse to make them clear is to refuse to believe in advance and improvement.

Grammatical or functional syllabuses?

Because learners receive most of their contact with the target language in the classroom, there has been more discussion of syllabus organisation for foreign language learners than for others. But such discussion has tended to concentrate on the linguistic organisation, whereas, for obvious reasons, second language and mother tongue teachers have been more concerned with what kind of things are being said rather than how they are said.

Until recently, it was universally assumed that when we taught language we were primarily teaching a system of grammar and pronunciation, together with a large number of vocabulary items. No-one, of course, would deny that good language users do have abilities in such areas, but it is certainly not clear that all learners benefit from consciously learning these things. Yet in any syllabus planning, we have the difficulty of how to organise what we are doing. That is, we have to decide:

a. what kind of units are appropriate for analysing our material;
b. what are the appropriate items to select for our particular students;
c. what is the best order to present these items in, which means deciding
d. what criteria of difficulty we are using.

Let us try to clarify what it means to fulfil all these requirements.

However clear we may be about what we want to teach, a syllabus must reflect some idea of how students learn. But in language teaching it is difficult to do this, because we know very little about the learning process. If we assume for the moment that we are thinking of language as grammar, pronunciation and vocabulary, how would this work out in relation to the above four areas of decision?

a. The units we have to deal with are vocabulary items, grammatical items and pronunciation items—and these will need defining in relation to our understanding of such linguistic categories.
b. Which items to select will depend on a definition of the needs of our students—what they will need the language for. If they are going to be tourists, then they will need to be able to use certain

vocabulary items, to produce reasonably understandable English, and to be able to understand a range of colloquial registers. If they are going to study in English at a university, their needs will be different, as they will be again if they are simply learning 'general English' early in their school careers, or if they are learning in order to be able to read English literature.

c. But as soon as we want to consider ordering we shall find that the problem of selection is more complicated than simply the definition of needs. Because, as language is a complex combination of systems, we cannot simply practise the things that students will eventually need to do. Indeed, experience suggests that we learn language very indirectly and we may need to practise things in class which assist learning of the final product but which are not the final product themselves. That is, we may need to become familiar with many language items which we may not eventually use all that much, as a means of acquiring the language system so that we can use it fluently and flexibly. So students who have had varied practise in using the language in different situations and settings will be able to operate as tourists more effectively than those who have only been introduced to the language of tourism. And the ordering will be determined by what helps us to learn as well as by what is close to our needs at the end of the course.

d. Thus there are varied criteria for difficulty. We may want to argue that some linguistic structures, some grammatical items, are by their internal organisation more complex, and consequently more difficult to learn, than others. We may want to argue that everyday items, however complicated, are easier to learn than uncommon ones. We may want to say that students will learn grammatical items which are closest to those of their own language, or ones which express ideas which interest them. So we appear to look at the idea of difficulty from a whole range of different points of view.

As these notes should make clear, it is impossible to separate decisions about course design from decisions about how our students learn.

One of the few firm statements that we can make about learning is that it is systematic. Both research and teaching experience suggest that we do not simply learn language items (except to some extent with vocabulary, though even this is learnt in relation to a semantic system), but we learn systems which produce language items in combination. Consequently our syllabus design should reflect the systems which underly language. And the most fundamental system is the grammatical one, for on the basis of a small number of grammatical rules we can produce a very large number of sentences, which we can use for a wide range of different language uses. It is for reasons such as these that grammatical bases for syllabuses have been preferred for many years.

However, to have a grammatical basis for a syllabus is not to say that the syllabus consists entirely of grammar, or that learners need to be aware of the grammatical basis. The syllabus specifies what the *teacher* is aware of, in order to ensure that coverage of the basic elements of the language is systematic. There have been syllabuses in the past which consisted of grammatical rules to the exclusion of almost everything else—much Latin teaching used such syllabuses. It should be noted, also, that many good language learners prefer to teach themselves by consciously learning the grammatical system in isolation when they approach a new language. But such methods assume a high degree of linguistic sophistication and motivation. For most learners a more immediate payoff is essential, and many good learners use methods which involve a close integration between language and use. In most formal learning situations, a grammatical syllabus will be unsatisfactory on its own because we do not propose to teach the grammar in isolation. In recent years there have been several attempts to find alternative bases for syllabus design, but— while a number of interesting and helpful proposals have emerged —none of them has produced an entirely successful syllabus.

It has been pointed out that we do not use language, usually, to show off our grammar, but to express meanings or to do things. So the most convincing basis for a new type of syllabus might be in terms of notions—that is, meaning elements, or functions, or elements based on what we do with language. It has also been suggested that we can construct syllabuses round the situations or settings in which students need to use the language they are learning.

No sensible person would claim that learning a language does not involve using it to express meanings, to do things effectively and to operate in situations. Any language teaching must enable these things to occur. But to say this is not to say that they should provide the basis, as distinct from the elements, of syllabus design. A syllabus must be adapted to the specific requirements of learners, but its central basis must be the essential characteristics of language which have to be learnt, organised in the way which will most assist learners. Thus the major elements of the linguistic system will be necessary, but so also will a whole range of other features which cannot be easily systematised—including a range of appropriate uses of language (apologising, asking for information, talking to officials, using language appropriate for shops, private houses, customs sheds). However, we cannot avoid requiring students to master some form of grammar of the language, even if it is a limited one, and our presentation must recognise this fact. In the past, most course books have recognised that criteria for the selection of materials include functional and notional as well as grammatical, pronunciation, vocabulary, and interesting content decisions. Because language learning is so complex, the process of course design will be complex. There will be no simple solutions, and good foreign language syllabuses will probably always be basically grammatical, and at the same time practically functional.

Mother tongue and second language syllabuses

We have seen that foreign language syllabuses tend to concentrate, at least in the first instance, on the formal characteristics of the target language. Such a procedure would be inappropriate in mother tongue and second language situations, for the target language is already known to some extent, and students will always be surrounded by language outside the class.

But as soon as we consider the other elements mentioned in discussing foreign language syllabuses, we can see that essentially the same principles can apply in all language teaching contexts. Students will always need to have their ranges of language use extended in relation to new situations, new content and increasingly sophisticated types of language use. Even if they are not made explicit, such assumptions underlie the organisation of teaching round topics and the relating of language work to other curriculum areas. In second language teaching, some overt presentation may still be necessary, depending on the gap between student performance and the target being offered, but in most situations the basic structure of the language can be taken for granted and the extension is part of an extension of social and cognitive awareness. Nonetheless, for the teacher, a clarification of the exact range of types of speech and writing, of the kind of audiences appropriate, of the various skills

151

and sub-skills required, and of the relations between language for understanding and language for production by students, is essential, and it is this clarification that a syllabus should provide.

Course design and professional activity

The discussion of course design has centred on syllabus organisation, because all institutions teaching languages require a syllabus as a basis for their courses. We have already referred to the ways in which a syllabus, by making explicit underlying principles, enables teaching to improve through discussion, criticism and revision. It also, of course, performs an administrative function by relating the work of various classes to each other, by ensuring continuity, not only from class to class but as teachers change over in the same class, and by providing succinct documentation of the work of the institution for outside use. Both the professional and the administrative functions of the syllabus are central to the effectiveness of any well-organised school, for through these the language work can be looked at whole, and on this basis the development of improved teaching can take place. The ideal situation, in fact, is that where the courses for the whole school are designed co-operatively by all teaching staff, so that the process of syllabus revision is continuous, and incorporates a constant self-assessment and self-improvement by the teachers. Although this situation is unfortunately rare, it is highly desirable, for in this way the training of teachers becomes part of a continuing professional sensitivity, closely related to the realities of teaching and students.

Training teachers

15 What training does a language teacher need?

In an ideal world, training of teachers, development of syllabuses and materials, teaching and inspection would be closely integrated. Few countries have even aspired to this ideal, and most people's training begins and ends, if it happens at all, before they start teaching seriously. Our discussion here will be primarily concerned with the central issue of teacher training, the integration of theory and practice. But it should be borne in mind that such integration can best be achieved by a close relationship between researchers and academics in education, trainers, and practising teachers, with the education of teachers occurring throughout their professional lives.

Learning about teaching

We learn about teaching in a wide range of different ways, for it is, as we have seen, a very complex activity. A great deal of what we learn we can only learn by doing, for learning to teach, like learning a language, is learning to perform in relation to other people. But it differs from language learning in that there is much to be gained from working alongside an experienced and sympathetic professional and discussing the details of the teaching process. A great deal of teaching can be acquired by apprenticeship.

However, teaching is not simply something that can be intuitively picked up by unstructured contact, for a lot of our teaching is highly conscious and thought out, and requires careful analysis if we are to be fully effective—and of course there are also a large number of contributions to be made to language teaching by disciplines like linguistics which are not primarily concerned with teaching at all.

A preparatory programme for language teaching, then, will

155

provide opportunities for students to develop skills, to increase their knowledge and understanding, and to do so in a way that enables them to operate effectively in the classroom with what they have learnt. It will also attempt to develop in students professional attitudes which are both realistic and committed.

Skills may be developed both systematically and unsystematically. Careful preparation of teaching, to be 'taught' to fellow-students in small groups, or to small groups of genuine pupils (microteaching), may provide opportunities for development of particular skills such as presentation of specific language items, or questioning, or opening free conversation. This may be planned and organised according to a careful syllabus, and may be videotaped and discussed, and possibly taught again, as a result of the discussion, in a revised form. Similarly, there may be highly controlled visits to schools where students may teach single lessons, or parts of lessons. And all this work will be accompanied by observation and discussion by tutors and fellow-students. Finally, an extended period should be taught in a school, with the help of support from the teaching staff and the tutor, so that work can be carried on fairly realistically with full responsibility for an extended sequence of lessons with at least one class. There is no effective alternative to the combination of thinking, planning, doing and discussing which results from procedures such as these, and a course which prepares teachers with no activity such as this is lacking its most important component.

But teaching is a great deal more than merely possessing skills. It requires careful thought to produce well planned schemes of work, well constructed lessons, and appropriate materials. Nor can thinking on its own be enough, for it is necessary to be well informed, and to understand the nature of language and of language learning as fully as possible. Indeed, a good language teacher will need to be aware of a great deal of discussion of general educational and philosophical issues, for, as we have seen, the development of language ties in very closely with general educational and cultural development. All of these are necessary aspects of an initial teacher's professional training.

Workshops, lectures and discussion can help trainee teachers to acquire the intellectual support necessary for a successful start in language teaching. The development of positive professional attitudes requires teacher trainers to be sensitive to another dimension, for this is something more likely to emerge from the approach—and indeed from the personal behaviour—of tutors than from any other single factor. Tutors, and the teachers in teaching practice schools, need to demonstrate the highest professional commitment themselves. They need to show to their students the same degree of sensitivity that they demand of the students in their relations with their pupils. The structure of the course should be as sensitive to student needs, and the methodology of the teacher training course as adaptable to individual student needs as the language syllabuses which are being recommended. With due allowances being made for important differences, a teacher training programme should reflect all the virtues that it claims to teach. It should not be necessary to have to say something as obvious as this, but unfortunately teacher training courses are too often academic and insensitive, and the point needs to be made firmly. Successful teacher training is very difficult, for it has to combine high academic standards with efficient development of practical skills, and good pastoral care, for students correctly understand that being a teacher is not simply using a new set of skills, but an expression of our most characteristic human capacities, intellectual, imaginative, moral and emotional. Learning to teach is never easy, least of all to the conscientious student, and most people find their initial training and early classroom experience the most stressful part of their whole career. Organisers of teacher training courses need to recognise and respond to this.

This is not the place to outline a full teacher training programme, but it is worth making one central point. Teachers at the beginning of their careers want to learn how to teach, and are consequently impatient of too much emphasis on contributory disciplines. Of course, good teaching requires understanding of much outside teaching, but on an initial training programme it is essential that the relationship between external knowledge and skilled teaching is made as explicit as possible. The course should not simply be about practical advice, for it is difficult to generalise from specific hints; nor should it be entirely a description of principles, for inexperienced teachers cannot be expected to see the significance of a principle until they have 'felt' it through experience in a classroom; but it should be about, and should exemplify in its structure and teaching mode, the *relationship* between principles and practice. Only out of such a training will teachers emerge who are principled in their practice and practical in their principles.

In-service training

We have already touched on the important issues here in several places earlier in this chapter. In-service training is all too frequently seen as a way of introducing teachers to the latest fashion, and implicitly of condemning their earlier practice. It is certainly true that teachers do wish to be introduced to new ideas, and in-service work has a clear role in this activity, but there is a much more important side to it. The teaching profession needs people who are constantly examining their work and experimenting with small-scale improvements, people who are thinking about their own and their colleagues' practice and publicly discussing the results of their thinking. There is a place for speculative discussion and for formal research in language teaching, but teaching should be informed by such scholarly activity, not dictated by it. And conversely, researchers and academics need constantly to be reminded of classroom realities, for their work, ultimately, is valuable insofar as it is applicable to classrooms as they really are, not to some idealised stereotype. The more careful and serious classroom-based discussion there is, and the closer the liaison between different people working in education, the more likely there is to be a truly effective teaching profession. Such a development is most likely to emerge from a consistent programme of in-service activity within the schools, centred on teachers, but calling on other appropriate organisations whenever necessary.

Conclusion

Much of what has been said about teacher training is not specific to language teaching. But this is as it should be, for language teaching is necessarily part of the educational system, and language teaching decisions need to be taken within a broader framework of the aims of education and ultimately of the kind of society we wish to become. This book has attempted to outline what language teachers should know about language and how it operates in the world, and to relate this to the central issues in language teaching theory and practice. This, in itself, presupposes a particular attitude to language teaching, and to teaching, on our part. Teaching is so bound up with the personal and social needs of particular groups of people, and is so central to the whole process of living in society, that we cannot ever expect neat, straightforward solutions to our problems. Furthermore, as language is so central to the establishment and maintenance of human relationships, language teaching will never emerge as an easily-definable problem with agreed solutions. But we can make use of what we do know to ensure that our discussions are well informed and principled.

This book has been written as a contribution to that process, but it can only be a beginning. Each reader will find, in teaching, more problems arising, more interesting issues to explore, and—no doubt—grounds for disagreeing with, or expanding on, points raised here. The final chapter, therefore, is a follow-up reading list, annotated, to enable readers to pursue further whatever lines of enquiry are most relevant to their own needs.

16 Professional development: further reading

For many people it is difficult to follow up an introductory book such as this one. The purpose of this final chapter is to give some indication of the most important and the most easily available materials to help those who want to extend their understanding of language and language teaching after reading each of the foregoing chapters. We shall try to offer two major types of information here:

1. reliable standard books to extend the ideas presented in this one;
2. sources of further information—including bibliographies and survey articles—to help those who may want to order materials for libraries and resource centres, or who simply want a map of the whole field in order to choose what areas to investigate further.

Basic books
NOTE: We have deliberately restricted the number of books referred to, but all those mentioned are reliable and clear. Unless otherwise mentioned, the place of publication is London.

Chapter One: on language, and on relating our understanding of language to language teaching
Four general introductions to the whole field of linguistics, in ascending order of difficulty, are:
JEAN AITCHISON, *Linguistics* (Teach Yourself Books), Hodder & Stoughton, second edition, 1978. A very simple and clear introduction to all important aspects of linguistics.
V. FROMKIN and R. RODMAN, *An Introduction to Language*, New York, Holt Rinehart & Winston, second edition, 1978. An entertaining and comprehensive introduction to linguistics.

MARTIN ATKINSON, DAVID KILBY and IGGY ROCA, *Foundations of General Linguistics*, George Allen & Unwin, 1982.

D. BOLINGER, *Aspects of Language*, New York, Harcourt Brace Jovanovich, third edition, 1980. The standard undergraduate introduction to linguistics; authoritative and comprehensive.

It is advisable to buy the latest edition of basic books on linguistics, as earlier editions may not reflect important recent developments.

Two basic books which integrate linguistic ideas with ideas drawn from other disciplines as a basis for language work in schools are:
(with a mother tongue bias) J. BRITTON, *Language and Learning*, Allen Lane, The Penguin Press, 1970 (also available as a Pelican).
(with a foreign language bias) S. PIT CORDER, *Introducing Applied Linguistics*, Penguin, 1973.

An influential attempt to relate linguistic principles to language work is:

M. A. K. HALLIDAY, A. MCINTOSH and P. STREVENS, *The Linguistic Sciences and Language Teaching*, Longman, 1964. Although quite demanding for the beginner, this is still well worth reading.

For more advanced work, a clear account of linguistics related to foreign and second language teaching can be found in the papers in Volumes II and III of *The Edinburgh Course in Applied Linguistics*, edited by J. P. B. ALLEN et al., Oxford University Press, 1974–5. There is no work at a comparable level relating to mother tongue teaching.

Finally, three more speculative works may be mentioned, each of which, in different ways, tries to build up a picture of the nature of language teaching on the basis of theory, in an effort to improve current practice:

PETER DOUGHTY, *Language, 'English' and the Curriculum*, Edward Arnold, 1974. This attempts to define the role of mother tongue English teaching in relation to theory.

EARL W. STEVICK, *Memory, Meaning and Method*, Rowley, Mass., Newbury House, 1976. This is a persuasive interpretation of psychological and linguistic research to argue the case for a more 'whole person' approach to foreign language teaching.

H. G. WIDDOWSON, *Teaching Language as Communication*, Oxford University Press, 1978. An argument for a greater concentration on the way language is used rather than on its formal properties.

Chapter Two: on syntax
A very clear account of all the major issues is:
FRANK PALMER, *Grammar*, Pelican, 1971. (And see also the four introductions mentioned under Chapter One.)

The standard reference grammar is:
R. QUIRK et al., *Grammar of Contemporary English*, Longman, 1972. No library should be without this. A shorter version suitable for reference by teachers is:
R. QUIRK and S. GREENBAUM, *University Grammar of English*, Longman, 1973, and this has a workbook:
R. A. CLOSE, *A University Grammar of English Workbook*, Longman, 1974.

An attempt to outline this grammar in functional terms has been made in:
G. LEECH and J. SVARTVIK, *A Communicative Grammar of English*, Longman, 1975.

Chapter Three: on phonology and phonetics
A clear and cheap account can be found in:
J. D. O'CONNOR, *Phonetics*, Pelican, 1973. (And in the four basic introductions.)

The standard account of the sound system of English is:
A. C. GIMSON, *An Introduction to the Pronunciation of English*, Edward Arnold, third edition, 1979.

A good, simple account aimed at foreign learners is:
J. D. O'CONNOR, *Better English Pronunciation*, Cambridge University Press, 1967.

A straightforward account of acoustic phonetics can be found in:
P. B. DENES and E. N. PINSON, *The Speech Chain*, New York, Bell Telephone Laboratories, 1963.

Chapter Four: on semantics
A straightforward initial text is:
FRANK PALMER, *Semantics*, Cambridge University Press, 2nd edn., 1981.

Another easily available book, more difficult than Palmer's, but wide-ranging and speculative, and fascinating reading, is:
G. LEECH, *Semantics*, Pelican, second edition, 1982.

The fullest advanced academic account of the contemporary scene in semantics, though even this is not comprehensive, is:
JOHN LYONS, *Semantics*, Cambridge University Press, 2 volumes, 1977.

Chapter Five: on sociolinguistics
There are several good introductions to sociolinguistics. In ascending order of difficulty these are:
PETER TRUDGILL, *Sociolinguistics*, Pelican, 1974.
ROGER BELL, *Sociolinguistics*, Batsford, 1976.
R. A. HUDSON, *Sociolinguistics*, Cambridge University Press, 1980.

Two excellent short books which relate sociolinguistic aspects to education are:
M. STUBBS, *Language, Schools and Classrooms*, Methuen, 1976 and
PETER TRUDGILL, *Accent, Dialect and School*, Edward Arnold, 1975.
Both of these should be read by all teachers.

Chapter Six: on stylistics
There are no real introductions to stylistics, but a simple initial account of language in literature can be found in:
RAYMOND CHAPMAN, *Linguistics and Literature*, Edward Arnold, 1973.

A more advanced consideration of linguistic problems in describing varieties of language can be found in:
D. CRYSTAL and D. DAVY, *Investigating English Style*, Longman, 1969.

A convenient short introduction to structuralist critics is:
T. HAWKES, *Structuralism and Semiotics*, Methuen, 1977.

Finally, the only full-length discussion of stylistics and education:
H. G. WIDDOWSON, *Stylistics and the Teaching of Literature*, Longman, 1975.

Chapter Seven: on psycholinguistics
JEAN AITCHISON, *The Articulate Mammal*, Hutchinson, 1976, is a racy introduction to psycholinguistics, providing very entertaining as well as informative reading.

DAN I. SLOBIN, *Psycholinguistics*, Scott, Foresman, 2nd edn., 1979, is a more conventionally-written book which also remains a useful introduction.

A good short account of language in relation to thinking is:
JUDITH GREENE, *Thought and Language*, Methuen, 1975.
MARGARET DONALDSON, *Children's Minds*, Collins, Fontana, 1978, is a clear and persuasive account of the development of concepts in relation to language and education activity, and includes important criticism of some of Piaget's experiments.

J. P. DE CECCO, (ed.), *The Psychology of Language, Thought and Instruction*, New York, Holt, Rinehart and Winston, 1969. This collection of readings is for the slightly more advanced reader. It provides a large number of important and useful papers, including several on language.

For the more advanced reader still, interested in the emergence of modern psycholinguistics, a book which retains its interest is:
LEON A. JAKOBOVITS and MURRAY S. MIRON, (eds.), *Readings in the Psychology of Language*, Prentice-Hall, 1967.

On the question of *second* language acquisition versus second language learning, a book which has recently become essential, though controversial, reading is:
STEPHEN D. KRASHEN, *Second Language Acquisition and Second Language Learning*, Pergamon, 1981.

Chapter Eight: on foreign language learning and teaching
There is a large number of useful introductions to foreign or second language teaching, especially with reference to the teaching of English overseas. Two useful general books on foreign language teaching are:
WILGA RIVERS, *Teaching Foreign-Language Skills*, Chicago, University of Chicago Press, 2nd edn., 1981.
ALAN HORNSEY (ed.), *A Handbook for Modern Language Teachers*, Methuen, 1975.

A book which summarises the behaviourist and mentalist approaches to language teaching and shows the tension between them in terms of teaching methods, as well as serving as a comprehensive introduction to many aspects of language teaching, is:

KENNETH CHASTAIN, *The Development of Modern Language Skills: Theory to Practice*, Philadelphia, Pa., The Center for Curriculum Development, 1971.

Books, all very accessible to beginners, on teaching English are:
J. A. BRIGHT and G. P. MCGREGOR, *Teaching English as a Foreign Language*, Longman, 1970. This relates particularly to teaching in African secondary schools, but contains an enormous wealth of ideas with wider application.
G. BROUGHTON et al., *Teaching English as a Foreign Language*, Routledge & Kegan Paul, 1978. A comprehensive overview.
MARY FINOCCHIARO, *Teaching English as a Second Language*, New York, Regent, second edition, 1974. An American perspective.
DONN BYRNE (ed.), *English Teaching Perspectives*, Longman, 1980. A wide-ranging book of extracts, all accessible to beginners.
MARIANNE CELCE-MURCIA and LOIS MCINTOSH (eds.), *Teaching English as a Second or Foreign Language*, Rowley, Mass., Newbury House, 1979. An excellent and comprehensive symposium, with much practical information.
WILGA RIVERS and MARY TEMPERLEY, *A Practical Guide to the Teaching of English as a Second or Foreign Language*, New York, Oxford University Press, 1978.
It is well worth the while of all language teachers to look at all these books, for there are no ideas which have relevance only to the type of teaching for which they have been devised.

As an introduction to ESP (and specific-purpose language teaching generally) a most useful collection is:
SUSAN HOLDEN, (ed.), *English for Specific Purposes*, Modern English Publications, 1977.
For communicative techniques, see:
WILLIAM LITTLEWOOD, *Communicative Language Teaching*, Cambridge University Press, 1981—a most readable introductory text, with many ideas for classroom techniques.
ALAN MALEY and ALAN DUFF, *Drama Techniques in Language Learning*, Cambridge University Press, 1978—again a most useful source of ideas.
KEITH JOHNSON and KEITH MORROW (eds.), *Communication in the Classroom*, Longman, 1980. This collection requires a little more familiarity with the theoretical issues, but is wide-ranging and stimulating.

For 'humanistic' or 'whole-person' techniques, see initially Stevick's book, *Memory, Meaning and Method*, mentioned under Chapter One. Stevick has followed this up with a further book—*Teaching Languages: A Way and Ways*, Rowley, Mass., Newbury House, 1980, but it should be read strictly as a sequel. Both books contain references to the works of Gattegno, Curran and Lozanov, who might be followed up individually at a later date.

On individualisation, perhaps the most accessible texts remain:
REBECCA M. VALETTE and RENÉE S. DISICK, *Modern Language Performance Objectives and Individualization*, Harcourt Brace Jovanovich, 1972.
RENÉE S. DISICK, *Individualizing Language Instruction*, Harcourt Brace Jovanovich, 1975.

Chapter Nine: on mother tongue learning and teaching
The clearest statement of a contemporary position on teaching English as a mother tongue is:
JOHN DIXON, *Growth through English*, Oxford University Press, third edition, 1975.
More theoretical discussion can be found in:
JAMES MOFFETT, *Teaching the Universe of Discourse*, Boston, Houghton Mifflin, 1968.
STEVEN TEN BRINKE, *The Complete Mother-tongue Curriculum*, Longman, 1976.

A broad discussion of the contemporary scene in Britain is available in:
A Language for Life, the Report of the Committee of Inquiry appointed by the Secretary of State for Education and Science under the chairmanship of Sir Alan Bullock, Her Majesty's Stationery Office, 1975. In spite of being an official report, this is interesting, readable and informative.

At a more practical level, see JAMES BRITTON (ed.), *Talking and Writing*, Methuen, 1967. Ideas in this are extended more theoretically in DOUGLAS BARNES et al., *Language, the Learner and the School*, revised edition, Penguin, 1971.

For the history of mother tongue teaching in Britain (English only):

DAVID SHAYER, *The Teaching of English in Schools 1900-1970*, Routledge & Kegan Paul, 1972.

For mother tongues other than English in Britain:
C. V. JAMES (ed.), *The Older Mother Tongues of the United Kingdom*, Centre for Information on Language Teaching and Research, 1978.
Bilingualism and British Education: the Dimensions of Diversity, CILT Reports and Papers 14, Centre for Information on Language Teaching and Research, 1976.

Bernstein's work is discussed in the two books by Stubbs and Trudgill at the end of the references under Chapter Five. His own writings, which make quite difficult reading, are collected in the three volumes of *Class, Codes and Control*, Routledge & Kegan Paul, 1971, 1973 and 1975. Discussion on literacy, acquisition, comprehension, linguistics and education can be found in two books:
RONALD WARDHAUGH, *Topics in Applied Linguistics*, Rowley, Mass., Newbury House, 1974.
BERNARD SPOLSKY, *Educational Linguistics*, Rowley, Mass., Newbury House, 1978.

Chapter Ten: on second language learning and teaching
Several books already referred to under Chapter Eight are relevant here, especially Bright and McGregor, and Finocchiaro, but for the second language situation in Britain there are no really satisfactory basic texts. The two books written particularly for this situation are both rather dated:
JUNE DERRICK, *Teaching English to Immigrants*, Longman, 1966.
JOHN and FRANCES STODDART, *The Teaching of English to Immigrant Children*, University of London Press, 1968.
An American book, MURIEL SAVILLE-TROIKE, *Foundations for Teaching English as a Second Language*, New Jersey, Prentice-Hall, 1976, says little which is not in the standard foreign language books. However, there is a useful book aimed at ESL tutors:
SANDRA NICHOLLS and JULIA NAISH, *Teaching English as a Second Language*, British Broadcasting Corporation, 1981.

Back issues of the journal *Multi-Racial School* (now NAME Journal: see the last section of this chapter) provide a useful source of information and discussion in this area.

Chapter Eleven: on psychology and language teaching
Undoubtedly the most relevant follow-up reading both to this chapter and to some extent to Chapter Seven, though it does make certain demands of the reader, is:
STEVEN H. MCDONOUGH, *Psychology in Foreign Language Teaching*, George Allen & Unwin, 1981.

A clear general introduction to the psychology of education is:
E. STONES, *Introduction to Educational Psychology*, Methuen, 1966.

J. RICHARDS (ed.), *Error Analysis*, Longman, 1974, is a collection of papers which provides further background on the notion of interlanguage.

An interesting collection of readings for those wishing to go further into the question of the effects of puberty on language learning capability as well as into other related issues (and a book which makes easier reading than its title suggests) is:
MARK LESTER (ed.), *Readings in Applied Transformational Grammar*, Holt, Rinehart & Winston, 1970.

A further collection of papers, now dated in some respects, but very interesting and wide-ranging in scope, is contained in:
PAUL PIMSLEUR and TERENCE QUINN (eds.), *The Psychology of Second Language Teaching*, Cambridge University Press, 1971.

Chapter Twelve: on testing
The standard, historical work in this field is:
ROBERT LADO, *Language Testing*, Longman, 1961. But this is very dated now.
Probably the most comprehensive overview is:
R. M. VALLETTE, *Modern Language Testing: a Handbook*, New York, Harcourt Brace Jovanovich, second edition 1977.
A book which still has much to offer is:
DAVID HARRIS, *Testing English as a Second Language*, New York, McGraw Hill, 1969.
Also worth looking at:
J. B. HEATON, *Writing English Language Tests*, Longman, 1975.
There have been several works published since these, but they are generally too tendentious for introductory reading.

All the above relate to foreign or second language learning. The testing of the mother tongue has not received an authoritative overview.

Chapter Thirteen: on technology in language teaching and learning
Probably still the best and most comprehensive introduction to the
application of educational technology in language teaching is:
J. B. HILTON, *Language Teaching: A Systems Approach*, Methuen,
1973.

Specific introductions to the language laboratory and its use tend to
date back to the 1960s, when the laboratory was more novel than it
is now. Two books still worth looking at, if available, are:
J. B. ADAM and A. J. SHAWCROSS, *The Language Laboratory*, Pitman,
1963.
J. D. TURNER, *Introduction to the Language Laboratory*, University
of London Press, 1965.
If one is acquainted with the basic mechanics of the laboratory, a
book which remains a classic in relation to its exploitation and use is:
JULIAN DAKIN, *The Language Laboratory and Language Teaching*,
Longman, 1973.

For visual aids and television, see:
RICHARD SHERRINGTON, *Television and Language Skills*, Oxford
University Press, 1973.
S. PIT CORDER, *The Visual Element in Language Teaching*, Long-
man, 1966.
ANDREW WRIGHT, *Visual Materials for the Language Teacher*,
Longman, 1976.

ELT Documents 105, *The Use of the Media in English Language
Teaching*, The British Council, 1979, is also an interesting collection
of papers on the application of radio and television to language
teaching and learning.

Chapter Fourteen: on course design and teacher training
General discussions of course design can be found particularly in two
books referred to under Chapter One: Pit Corder, *Introducing
Applied Linguistics*, and *The Edinburgh Course in Applied Linguistics*. A fairly academic account of current assumptions about second
and foreign language course design can be found in C. J. BRUMFIT
and K. JOHNSON (eds), *The Communicative Approach to Language
Teaching*, Oxford University Press, 1979. For an account of
assumptions of the 1960s, see:
W. F. MACKEY, *Language Teaching Analysis*, Longman, 1965.

For functional syllabuses (one side of the argument only) see D. A. WILKINS, *Notional Syllabuses*, Oxford University Press, 1976.

There is very little good general discussion of teacher training for language teaching. A recent collection, which touches on a number of important points is:

S. HOLDEN (ed.), *Teacher Training*, Modern English Publications, 1978.

Teaching practice is discussed in general in:

E. STONES and S. MORRIS, *Teaching Practice: Problems and Perspectives*, Methuen, 1972.

Microteaching is discussed in general in:

GEORGE BROWN, *Microteaching*, Methuen, 1975.

Extensive treatment of microteaching for language teaching can be found in K. CRIPWELL and M. GEDDES (eds), *Microteaching and EFL Teacher Training*, English as a Foreign Language Department, University of London Institute of Education, 1979.

Sources of further information

In some ways this is the most important section of the whole book, if the kind of professional development referred to in Chapter Fifteen is to be maintained. There are three main ways of continuing to remain in touch with ideas in the middle of the rush and strain of day to day teaching. One is through personal contacts, particularly associations of language teachers. The addresses of the major associations are given below, but in every area there will of course be local groups, and any committed teacher will wish to search them out, or—if necessary—help to found one. The second way is through libraries or other channels for obtaining bibliographical and other relevant information. Again, such sources will need to be found locally. The third way is through subscription to language teaching periodicals. Details of the most useful of these are given below.

Associations relevant to language teachers

The Centre for Information on Language Teaching (see below) issues a guide to national associations. Among others, there are associations for German, Italian, Russian, Spanish and Portuguese teachers. Other associations with wider concerns are:

British Association for Language Teaching, BALT (Mrs E. A. Dyson, Glanffrwd, Fernbrook Road, Penmaen Mawr, Gwynedd);

National Association for Multi-Racial Education, NAME (Ms M. Blakeley, 23 Doles Lane, Findern, Derbyshire D6 6AX);

National Association for the Teaching of English, NATE (10B Thornhill Road, Edgerton, Huddersfield HD3 3AU).

And at an academic level: British Association for Applied Linguistics (BAAL) (J. T. Roberts, Department of Language and Linguistics, University of Essex, Wivenhoe Park, Colchester CO4 3SQ).

All these associations are affiliated, together with many others, to the National Congress on Languages in Education. In addition, BAAL is affiliated to AILA (Association Internationale de Linguistique Appliquée) which has affiliate applied linguistics associations in most countries.

For mother tongues other than English, in Britain: Co-ordinating Committee for Mother Tongue Teaching, CCMMT (Roy Truman, Isledon Centre, Highbury Station Road, London N1 1SB).

International Association of Teachers of English as a Foreign Language, IATEFL (W. R. Lee, 16 Alexandra Gardens, Hounslow, Middlesex TW3 4HU);

National Association for Teaching English as a Second Language to Adults, NATESLA (c/o Greenwich Language Scheme, CCRE, Old Town Hall, Polytechnic Street, Woolwich SE18 6PN);

Teachers of English to Speakers of Other Languages, TESOL (James E. Alatis, Georgetown University, Washington D.C., U.S.A.).

IATEFL and TESOL are international organisations, TESOL having national affiliates, and IATEFL individual members in many countries.

Obviously we cannot list similar associations for all countries, but most countries do have groups such as these.

Libraries and Information sources

The most important source in Britain is CILT (The Centre for Information on Language Teaching and Research, 20 Carlton House Terrace, London SW1). This has a library which is shared with the English Language Teaching Services of the British Council, and produces bibliographies, surveys of research on language teaching, and abstracts of important new papers (published by Cambridge University Press, see below). For information about newly published textbooks it is usually necessary to contact individual publishers, though for English teaching to foreigners there is DELTA (66 York

Road, Weybridge, Surrey KT13 9ET) which publishes a newsletter and annual catalogue of English teaching books.

There will of course be local sources of information in most countries, particularly through British Council offices.

Language teaching periodicals
(in approximately ascending order of theoretical difficulty)

Modern English Teacher (Modern English Publications, P.O. Box 129, Oxford, OX2 8JU). EFL and ESL.

English Teaching Forum (available at US Embassies in countries where English is not a mother tongue). EFL and ESL.

World Language English (Pergamon Press, Headington Hill Hall, Oxford) EFL and ESL.

English Language Teaching Journal (Oxford University Press). EFL and ESL.

English in Education (NATE Office, Fernleigh, 10B Thornhill Road, Edgerton, Huddersfield HD3 3AU). Mother Tongue and some ESL occasionally.

The Use of English (Scottish Academic Press, 33 Montgomery Street, Edinburgh, Scotland). Mother Tongue and occasional ESL.

NAME—New Approaches to Multiracial Education (Journal of NAME, see above). ESL and general educational issues.

Commission for Racial Equality Education Journal (CRE, Elliot House, 10–12 Allington Street, London SW1E 5EH). ESL and general education.

ARELS Journal (Association of Recognised English Language Schools, 125 High Holborn, London WC1). EFL.

British Journal of Language Teaching (Journal of BALT, see above). Foreign Language Teaching.

ELT Documents (Pergamon Press, Headington Hill Hall, Oxford). EFL and ESL.

Educational Review (School of Education, Birmingham University). Occasional issues specifically on language and education.

System: A Journal for Educational Technology and Language Learning Systems (Pergamon Press).

TESOL Quarterly (Georgetown University, Washington D.C., USA). EFL and ESL.

Language Learning (University of Michigan, Ann Arbor, Michigan, USA).

Applied Linguistics (Oxford University Press).

In addition, every library should stock:

Language Teaching (Cambridge University Press). This not only includes abstracts of papers relating to language studies and language teaching, but also regularly updated annotated bibliographies, surveys of research in language teaching from all over Europe, and survey articles (one per issue) which summarise the state of current thinking, with extensive bibliographies, on all important areas. The first eleven of these surveys have been published in a book: V. KINSELLA (ed.), *Language Teaching and Linguistics: Surveys*, Cambridge University Press, 1978. (A further book is now in preparation.)

A reference to a book of survey articles is perhaps a good way to end the present book, for this is intended to be an introduction to the language teaching profession, and the survey articles indicate the many directions that our studies of language teaching can lead us into. Language is so centrally bound up with human variety and human needs that it will never lose either its importance or its fascination. We can only hope that our readers will find it as compelling a study as we have done ourselves.

Glossary of
linguistics and
language teaching
terms

Glossary of linguistics and language teaching terms

KEY: FL = foreign language
LT = language teaching
LL = language learning
TL = target language
* = ungrammatical, unacceptable, incorrect
(q.v.) = quod vide (which see)
cf. = compare

Where the term defined in an entry is used in context in this book, the chapter reference is given in brackets at the end of the entry.

NOTE: We have written this glossary for those beginning to find out more about language and language teaching and have therefore tried, as far as possible, to give definitions in everyday language rather than in technical terms. We hope not to mislead by doing this, but suggest that our definitions should only be regarded as a point of departure, and 'tightened up' in the light of advancing technical knowledge.

Accent Manner of pronunciation characteristic of a person or group, often indicating regional and/or social origin. A particular accent usually accompanies a particular *dialect* (q.v.), but does not in itself constitute a dialect. (11)

Accuracy Pronouncing a language and using its grammar and idioms in a manner acceptable to, and judged correct by, native speakers of the language; ability to use language in accordance with accepted norms. 'Accuracy' contrasts generally in context of LT today with 'fluency' (q.v.).

Achievement   A psychological and testing term referring to what an individual can demonstrate as having learnt, or having learnt to do. (11)

Acoustic   Referring to sound and hearing of sound. *Acoustic phonetics*—branch of phonetics concerned with physical properties of speech sounds. (1)

Active   The form of the verb (q.v.) indicating that it is the subject of the sentence that is performing the action or responsible for the event expressed by the verb (q.v.)—e.g. 'Jack *drank* the beer', 'Bill *felled* the tree' as opposed to 'The beer was drunk by Jack', 'The tree was felled by Bill'. Contrasts with 'passive' (q.v.).

Acquisition   See under *language acquisition* below.

Adjective   A word conveying a property of a person or thing—the *fat* man; the *blue* pencil; the *evil* idea. Adjectives may be *attributive*, placed before the person or thing to which they refer, or *predicative*, as in: the man is *ill*; the room seems *large*. In English and many other languages, not *all* adjectives can be used both attributively and predicatively—e.g. my previous house;* my house is previous. (7)

Adverb   A word or group of words which modifies (i.e. adds to or restricts the meaning of) a verb (q.v.), an adjective (q.v.), another adverb or a sentence (q.v.)—e.g. 'he ran *fast*', '*very* beautiful', '*extremely* badly,' 'they came *yesterday*'.

Affective   Referring to the feelings or emotions. *Affective aspects* of LL—those aspects involving the feelings. (cf. *cognitive*). (11)

Affricate   Sound perceived in a language as combination of stop (q.v.) and fricative (q.v.)—e.g. the *ch* (tš) of *church*. (3)

Agreement   The consistency, or harmony, between the parts of speech in a sentence as required by a particular language—e.g. in standard English 'The children *are* playing' demonstrates agreement between the plural (q.v.) noun and the plural form of the verb, whereas 'The children *is* playing' violates agreement. Agreement is also sometimes referred to as 'concord'. (2)

Aim/Aims   In LT/LL, what one wishes or needs to achieve in a particular course, or a statement of what one wishes or needs to achieve—e.g. 'The *aim* of the course is *fluency in spoken French*.' The term 'goal'/'goals' is often used in the same sense, as is 'objective'/'objectives'; but see also under *objective/objectives*. (8)

Allophone   One of several or many speech sounds representing a particular phoneme (q.v.)—e.g. in English, *l*ong [1] and lo*ll* [ɫ] are both allophones of /1/. (3)

Alveolar Describes a sound formed through contact between the tongue and the hard ridge behind the upper front teeth and forward of the soft palate, this ridge being the *alveolar ridge*. In English, [t] and [d] are *alveolar* consonants (q.v.). (3)

Analytic Describes approaches to LT in which there is no particular attempt to control the language to which learners are exposed in terms of ordering (q.v.) and grading (q.v.) or to 'predigest' language for the learners by breaking it down into rules. Contrasts with 'synthetic' (q.v.).

Anthropology The study of human beings in relation to their evolutionary development, culture, religion, social institutions, etc. (5)

Approach In LT the term is usually used to refer to a general view of how teaching should be carried out—e.g. 'oral approach' conveys that stress should be put on the spoken language. Though not everyone observes the distinction, 'approach' may often be taken to contrast with 'method' (q.v.) in that the latter is more concrete and precise—e.g. the Direct Method is a definite set of procedures, but stems from an 'oral approach'. (8)

Aptitude A psychological term referring to the *potential* of someone to do or learn something. (11)

Articulatory Referring to the *production* of speech sounds—e.g. *articulatory phonetics*—the branch of phonetics dealing with the production of speech sounds; *articulatory organs*—the parts of the body (mouth, tongue, larynx, etc.) used to produce speech. (1)

Aspect In essence, a way of looking at things. Some languages, such as English, can indicate through the form of the verb (q.v.) or through other parts of speech whether a speaker sees something as a *process* or a *state*, as a *present*, *ongoing* action or as a *habitual* action—e.g. 'He is having a good time' [*now*], versus: 'He *has* a good time' [every week, when he plays golf]. The English verb-system has both a *progressive* [be + . . . ing] and a *stative* aspect. (2)

Aspiration In phonetics, the emission of a puff of breath following the build-up and release of air-pressure—e.g. following the *p* in *pin*. Indicated in phonetic script by a small, superscripted 'h'—e.g. [p^{h}in]. (3)

Association In psychology, the process whereby a particular response (q.v.) becomes linked with, or learnt as, a habitual reaction to a particular stimulus (q.v.) (7)

Associative chain   A concept in behaviourist psychology (see under *behaviourism*) referring to the product of a process whereby one response is linked to another, this one to another, this one to another, and so on. (7)

Attainment   A psychological and testing term referring to what an individual has actually achieved by way of learning. Synonymous with 'achievement'. (12)

Attitude   In context of LL/LT generally used to refer to way in which learners view, evaluate and respond emotionally to TL and the society or societies in which it is spoken.

Audio-visual aids   Collective term for all technical LT aids such as tape and cassette recorders, slide, ciné and ciné-loop projectors, videotape recorders and TV monitors. (12)

Audiolingualism   An approach (q.v.) to LT popular in the 1960s, especially in the USA, and influenced by ideas stemming from structuralist linguistics (see under *structuralism*) and behaviourist psychology (see under *behaviourism*). According to this approach, there are four major language skills—Listening (understanding the spoken word), Speaking, Reading, Writing, to be presented and learnt in this order. It is also axiomatic to this approach that language be learnt through *imitation* and *practice* (q.v.), and a special feature of audiolingual teaching is the *pattern drill* (q.v.), intended to make the structural patterns of the TL part of the learner's linguistic 'habits'. (8)

Auditory discrimination   The ability to distinguish between sounds differing only slightly from each other. It has sometimes been suggested that this ability is a factor in (foreign) language learning aptitude (q.v.). (11)

Backwash   Testing term. Though it is usually assumed that achievement tests and examinations should be designed in accordance with what has been taught, it is known that things often happen the other way round, particularly with examinations which are set and sat regularly: in such cases, teaching may be adapted to the requirements of the examinations, and this process whereby the examinations influence the teaching is called 'backwash'. (12)

Battery   Testing term, used to refer to a complex test made up of several sub-tests.

Behaviourism   A school of psychology of particular influence in the earlier part of this century, especially in the field of education, and empiricist (see under *empiricism*) in its approach. Its focus is the behaviour of living organisms and the external factors which 'shape' this behaviour rather than 'inner states' or conditions of the mind. Behaviourist ideas were incorporated into the theoretical basis of audiolingualism (q.v.). (7, 11)

Biculturalism The state of belonging, or feeling that one belongs, more or less equally to two different cultures; being able to appreciate the cultural values of more than one society at the same time. (11)

Bilabial In phonetics, describes a sound produced with both lips—e.g. in English [p] and [b]. (3)

Bilingual In narrowest sense, describes people who can speak two languages, or countries in which two languages are spoken, but in relation to people is often used nowadays in the more general sense of 'not monolingual', i.e. not having only one language. Neither does the use of the term in relation to people necessarily mean that they have equal mastery of two languages (which is more properly referred to as 'equilingualism') but more usually simply that they use different languages in different areas of their lives.

CAL Abbreviation for Computer-Assisted Learning (q.v.).

Chomsky Noam Chomsky, b. 1928, American linguist (and political critic), Professor of Linguistics at Massachusetts Institute of Technology. Initiator of theory of language known as Transformational Generative Grammar (also referred to as 'Chomskyan linguistics'). His distinction between *competence* (q.v.) and *performance* (q.v.) has been highly influential in ideas about LT/LL (though Chomsky himself has always been cautious about the implications of linguistics for LT). His best-known work is *Aspects of the Theory of Syntax*. (7)

Cloze test Testing procedure in which a certain number of words—typically between every fifth and ninth—or certain categories of words—e.g. nouns or verbs—are deleted from a passage of continuous writing. Candidates being tested are presented with the passage containing the deletions and are required to supply the words deleted (or synonyms of the correct category). The theory is that the procedure simultaneously tests comprehension, lexical and structural knowledge, and the ability to 'reconstruct' the language. (12)

Cognition Psychological term for the process whereby knowledge is acquired; mental perception and reasoning. (7)

Cognitive Refers to cognition (q.v.). The *cognitive faculties*: the faculties, or powers, of intellectual learning and reasoning. *Cognitive factors*: in LL/LT, factors connected with learning, especially through application of the intellect (as opposed, for example, to *affective factors*—see also under *affective*, above). (11)

Collocation Grouping together of words or phrases, particularly customary groupings such as 'a hot tip', 'cool as a cucumber', 'a furtive glance'. (4)

Communicative approach Approach (q.v.) to LT which views language as a form of social behaviour and sees aim of LT as teaching learners to communicate fluently, appropriately and spontaneously in the cultural context of the TL. The prime source of ideas on which this approach rests is the *theory of communicative competence* (q.v.), whose initiator is generally accepted to have been the American sociolinguist and anthropologist Dell Hymes (q.v.). Hymes himself, however, was influenced by the prior work of other linguists and philosophers interested in language as a social tool. Much of the initial work on translating the theory of communicative competence into a LT approach was done under the aegis of the Council of Europe, notably by David Wilkins and J. Van Ek. The work of Henry Widdowson and John Munby has also been very influential in the development of the approach. In practical terms, the communicative approach has shifted the major focus of teaching away from structural aspects —though these are still regarded as important in effective communication—towards the cultivation of fluent and appropriate language. The communicative approach may be regarded as the currently 'orthodox' approach to the teaching of English as a foreign language. (8)

Communicative competence The ability to communicate through language fluently, spontaneously and appropriately within a given cultural context; the ability to engage in 'speech acts' (see under *speech act*). Though he may not have been the first to use the term, it is Dell Hymes (q.v.) who is generally credited with popularising the concept. (8)

Communicative needs The purposes for which a learner needs to know and use the TL in the context of communication. See also under *needs analysis*, below. (8, 11)

Communicative syllabus   A syllabus which, particularly by contrast with a grammatical syllabus (q.v.), aims to make learners communicatively competent (see under *communicative competence*) and is based on an analysis of the learners' communicative needs (q.v.). Usually synonymous with 'functional syllabus' (q.v.)

Communicative testing   Testing of a type which aims at testing the communicative competence (q.v.) of learners; which tests ability to use language rather than simply testing 'knowledge about it'.

Community Language Learning   An approach (q.v.) to LT/LL initiated by Charles Curran (q.v.) in the USA. As its name suggests, the approach emphasises the idea of 'community' between the learners, who typically sit in a close circle. The teacher is referred to as the 'knower' or 'counsellor' and assists the learners as the need arises. Transfer to the TL is gradual; initially dialogues and discussions commence in the native language, with the 'knower' supplying TL 'translations' then repeated by the learners. Inspired by ideas derived from counselling techniques, and also known as 'counselling learning'. (8)

Competence   In general sense, ability to perform in the TL. In technical sense, more precisely referred to as 'linguistic competence', i.e. the native speaker's tacit knowledge of the rules of his language. The notion stems from the work of Chomsky (q.v.), and contrasts with 'performance' (q.v.) as well as with 'communicative competence' (q.v.) (8)

Computer-assisted learning   Any system of teaching and learning which uses a computer to assist learners—e.g. through the presentation of material, the administering and scoring of tests and the keeping of records and giving of feedback (q.v.) on learners' progress etc. (13)

Concord   Another term for 'agreement' (q.v.) (2)

Conditional reflex   Reflex (q.v.) produced by conditioning (q.v.) (7)

Conditioning   Term associated with behaviourist psychology (see under *behaviourism*) for a process whereby a living organism is trained to respond habitually in a certain way to a given stimulus (q.v.) (7)

Consonants   Those speech sounds which are produced with *relative* blocking or closure of the mouth and nasal cavity (by contrast with vowels (q.v.)). The consonants of English are: p, b, t, d, č (as in *ch*urch), ǰ (as in *j*udge), k, g, f, v, θ (as in *th*in), ð (as in *th*at), s, z, š (as in *sh*oe), ž (as in *ge*nre), m, n, ŋ (as in si*ng*), l, r, j, w, h. (3)

Content word In grammar, a word which carries major meaning as opposed to a word which indicates grammatical relationships—e.g. 'the *boy went* to the *shop* to *buy* a *bag* of *sweets*'. Content words are usually considered to consist of the categories: noun (q.v.), verb (q.v.), adjective (q.v.), adverb (q.v.). (4)

Context In linguistics, the parts of a passage of writing or speech surrounding a particular word or particular sub-part of the passage, or, more broadly, the whole situation surrounding an instance of language use. (4)

Contrastive analysis The process, or product, of comparing and contrasting two or more languages in order to discover their similarities and differences. Contrastive analysis was central to Audiolingualism (q.v.) because it was assumed that the major learning difficulties would arise from the major differences between a learner's native language and the TL. (8)

Contrastive syntax, etc. The study of syntax from a contrastive viewpoint, i.e. with regard to the similarities and differences between two or more languages. Similar studies may also, of course, be undertaken in relation to other aspects of language, such as phonology and semantics. (2)

Copula Grammatical term for the 'joining' verb 'be'—e.g. 'Peter *is* in the bath'; 'Peter *is* doing his homework'. Sometimes thought of as an 'empty' verb—some languages, such as Russian, have no copula and would say the equivalent of 'Peter in bath', etc. (7)

Counselling learning See under *community language learning*, above.

Course design The process, or product, of planning a language course, including the drawing-up of a syllabus and the taking of decisions about teaching methods, etc. (14)

Creativity A psycholinguistic term for the potential of a speaker to create sentences and sentence-combinations which are 'novel' in the sense that the speaker has not learnt them off by heart, but has learnt the rules of his language, which allow him, in theory, to produce any and all of the sentences which are grammatical within it. (7)

Creole A language created out of the contact between two languages, such that it is neither, but possesses elements of both, and which serves as the mother tongue of the group speaking it. Contrasts with 'pidgin' (q.v.). (5)

Criterion-referenced test A test which aims to discover whether those tested can *use* or *do something with* the language being tested rather than merely demonstrate comprehension or ability to produce it. Such a test might, for example, require candidates to interpret a diagram and explain it; if they meet this criterion, rather than simply using language correctly, they will have performed adequately; accuracy (q.v.) may still, however, be an important factor in explaining the diagram, or in carrying out whatever task is set as a test, and may still distinguish between bare adequacy and a better performance. Contrasts with 'norm-referenced test' (q.v.). (12)

Culture In LT, was at one time taken to refer predominantly to the literary and artistic traditions of a society, but nowadays tends to be used in the wider, sociological sense to refer to everything which constitutes the background, history, traditions, behaviour and attitudes of a society.

Curran Charles A. Curran, founder of LT approach known as Community Language Learning (q.v.). Major LT publication: *Counseling Learning in Second Languages*. (8)

Curriculum The path of learning prescribed for a particular phase of education. Has a wider meaning than 'syllabus' (q.v.) because it refers to the totality of what is to be learnt and experienced during this phase rather than to the planning and organisation of any one particular subject. (14)

Declarative Describes the sentence-type used for making statements and assertions (as opposed to asking questions or giving commands)—e.g. 'the sun is shining today'; 'the sun rises every morning'.

Decoding The 'processing' in the brain of language heard or read in order to extract the meaning conveyed in it. cf. 'encoding', below. (7)

Deep structure Term from Transformational Generative Grammar (q.v.), in which it is proposed that a sentence may be assigned both a surface structure (q.v.) and a deep structure, this latter representing in effect the conceptual content or meaning of the sentence. (2)

Description A linguistic description, or description of a language, is an account which is intended to reflect, impartially and objectively, linguistic features as they actually are and not as it is thought they 'ought' to be. 'Description' often contrasts with 'prescription' (q.v.); by the same token, 'descriptive rules' contrast with 'prescriptive rules'. (2)

Developmental Psycholinguistics The branch of psycholinguistics (q.v.) which is concerned with the linguistic development of children. (7)

Diachronic The diachronic study of a language is one which examines its historical development. 'Diachronic' contrasts with 'synchronic' (q.v.) (1)

Diagnostic test A test administered to establish the state of a learner's knowledge of a language in order to plan remedial teaching where necessary and to ascertain what points this teaching should cover. (12)

Dialect A dialect is a regional or social variant (q.v.) of a language regarded both by the speakers of the dialect and by other speakers of the language as part of the language. Is usually taken to mean a non-standard variant of the language (see under *standard language*), though the standard form may also be referred to as 'the standard dialect'. (5)

Dictation A procedure used both for teaching and testing purposes whereby a passage is read out to a group of learners who have to write it down as they hear it. Though the pedagogical value of dictation has often been questioned, it has recently regained popularity as a form of integrative test (q.v.). (12)

Diphthong Phonetic term, referring to any vowel (q.v.) whose production is perceived as combining two separate vowels—e.g. the [ei] of the word 'late'. (3)

Direct Method LT method (q.v.) pioneered in the last third of the nineteenth century. Notable among its founders were W. Viëtor in Germany and Paul Passy in France. The method attempted to follow what seemed to be the 'natural' principles of children's language learning. It stressed that language should always first be presented orally, that grammar should be taught through 'object lessons' and association, that the mother tongue should not be used in the FL classroom, and interest in the culture of the TL should be actively encouraged. Was largely a direct reaction to the widespread use of the Grammar-Translation Method (q.v.) in school. (8)

Disabling Factor Any factor which makes it more difficult for a learner than it would otherwise be to learn a FL or benefit in some other way from schooling or education. Contrasts with 'enabling factor' (q.v.) (11)

Discourse Verbal and written communication generally; a text or part of a text, written or spoken, ranging over a number of sentences or utterances. (1)

Discrete Point Test   In LT, a test which breaks down aspects of a language into separate, self-contained units—e.g. word order, vocabulary, pronunciation—and tests knowledge of each point in isolation from others. Contrasts with 'integrative test' (q.v.) (12)

Discrimination   In testing, the degree to which a test discriminates, or separates out, candidates. A test which is so easy that everyone in a group can do it will discriminate little; likewise one that it is too difficult. Testing theorists advocate tests which discriminate sufficiently to produce a range of performances from good to poor in accordance with the principle of 'natural distribution'. (12)

Distinctive Feature   In phonology/phonetics, one of a set of features which serve to distinguish one language sound from another —e.g. the English [p] and [b] share all features which distinguish both of them from other English sounds, but are distinguished from each other by virtue of the fact that [p] is voiceless (q.v.) and [b] is voiced (q.v.), so that voice is the distinctive feature by which they differ. (3)

Diversity   The cultural and/or linguistic variety existing within a given country or community. (11)

Drill   A LT procedure designed to ensure assimilation of some linguistic point through repetition and usually also through manipulation, i.e. changing or modifying the linguistic elements presented in the drill. See also under *pattern drill*. (8)

Drive   Psychological term, more or less synonymous with 'motivation' (q.v.) (7)

Dynamic   A dynamic description (q.v.) of a language is one that attempts to capture language use in such a way as to show how it varies from individual to individual and group to group and how it changes from moment to moment. Contrasts with 'static' (q.v.). (5)

EAP   Abbreviation for 'English for Academic Purposes'. (8)

Eclecticism   An approach to LT which is essentially pragmatic, and advocates the judicious use of those parts of any LT methods which seem most useful and effective rather than sticking to one particular method or set of techniques for reasons of 'theoretical purism'.

Educational Technology   Education viewed as a technology, i.e. a system organised in accordance with scientific knowledge; the application to education of systematic planning and organisation utilising current scientific knowledge and technical aids (q.v.) (13)

EFL   Abbreviation for 'English as a Foreign Language'. (10)

Empirical Refers essentially to experience; in LL/LT usually met with in context of 'empirical research', i.e. research based on experimentation and observation as opposed to theorising or speculating. (5)

Empiricism Philosophical tendency to accept as valid only that knowledge which is derived from observation, experience and practice. In LL/LT context often intended as a synonym for 'behaviourism' (q.v.) and/or 'structuralism' (q.v.). (7)

Enabling Factor Any factor which makes it easier for a learner than it would be otherwise to learn a FL or benefit in some other way from schooling or education. Contrasts with 'disabling factor' (q.v.). (11)

Encoding The process within the brain of putting a message or meaning into a linguistic form so that it may be transmitted through speech or writing. cf. 'decoding', above. (7)

Error At one time this term could be applied arbitrarily and indiscriminately to any deviation from the linguistic norm (q.v.), but in recent years it has become more usual to apply it only to those 'mistakes' and deviations which can be traced back to the state of a learner's competence (q.v.) rather than to his performance (q.v.). Further, the term is no longer pejorative in LL/LT, since errors may be seen to demonstrate how learners are *progressing* in the FL, and are no longer simply interpreted as signs of 'failure to learn'. See also under *systematic error* and *random error*, below. (11)

Error Analysis The process, or product, of attempting to interpret errors made by learners in order to determine how well they are progressing in the learning of a FL, what problems they are experiencing, what the sources of their errors are, and what remedial teaching, if any, is necessary. (8)

ESL Abbreviation for 'English as a Second Language'. See also under *second language*, below. (10)

EST Abbreviation for 'English for Science and Technology'. (8)

Exponent In context 'exponents of language functions', the actual words and phrases used to express a function (q.v.). (8)

Exposure In LL/LT, usually refers to the arrangements for letting the learner come into contact with the TL, or the time during which the learner is exposed to the TL. (8)

Extinction The process whereby a once habitual response (q.v.) to a stimulus (q.v.) gradually dies through lack of reinforcement (q.v.); the point at which this occurs. (7)

EXTOL 'East Anglia and Essex Teaching Oriented Language'. A simple authoring language to assist non-computer-specialists to write computer-assisted instructional material. Potentially of great value to language teachers wishing to exploit the possibilities of computer-assistance. Developed by M. J. Kenning (University of Essex) and M. M. Kenning (University of East Anglia).

Feedback Information 'fed back' to the teacher from learners on questions such as the efficacy of the teaching and the materials, and in the light of which teaching arrangements can be modified and improved; information 'fed back' to learners to help them gauge their performance and progress.

Feel Judgement The spontaneous judgement made by a native speaker with regard to some aspect of the language such as grammar or style.

Fluency The ability to speak or write a language spontaneously, appropriately, and with adequate speed. In present-day LL/LT often intended to contrast with 'accuracy' (q.v.). (8)

Foreign Language Term usually applied only to languages spoken outside the boundaries of the country in which one lives, or, more crucially, to languages learnt only for communication with those living outside one's own community and not used for everyday communication within one's own community. cf. *second language*. (8)

Form In relation to language, the words used to express a message or idea, and the style in which it is expressed, rather than the message or idea itself. (7)

Formalism In literary criticism and stylistics (q.v.) concern with the form (q.v.) or linguistic structure of texts. (6). More generally in linguistics, the accepted conventions and forms through which arguments, rules etc. are expressed.

Fossilisation In error analysis (q.v.), term used for the process whereby learners retain certain errors irrespective of the amount of exposure to the TL or the amount of remedial teaching. The generally accepted explanation of fossilisation is that once learners have attained a communicative competence (q.v.) sufficient for their needs, they are no longer motivated to advance further towards adoption of the norms of the TL. (11)

Four Skills The major language skills as identified by Audiolingualism (q.v.): Listening (understanding the spoken word); Speaking; Reading (understanding the written word); Writing. According to audiolingual theory, Listening and Reading are *passive* or *receptive* skills, and Speaking and Writing *productive* skills. (8)

Fricative A consonant (q.v.) shaped by close approximation of or light pressure between articulatory (q.v.) surfaces such as upper teeth and lower lip and produced by the expulsion of air through the narrow channel formed. Literally, a 'rubbing' sound. Examples: [f] and [z]. (3)

Function The purpose for which a certain form of language is used; a category of purposive use of language—e.g. asking questions, making introductions, offering apologies. In recent years special attention has been given to functions following the realisation that form (q.v.) does not necessarily indicate function —e.g. a statement-form such as 'I'm lost' may not be a statement at all from a functional viewpoint, but in some situations a request for information, meaning 'Please tell me the way', etc. (8)

Functional Syllabus A syllabus (q.v.) which, instead of focusing on the grammar of a language, focuses on language functions (see under *function*) and which, in principle, provides only for the teaching of those aspects of grammar needed to express the particular functions taught. Contrasts with 'grammatical syllabus' (q.v.). (14)

Future The tense (q.v.) used to express future events—e.g. 'Sam *will do* the work tomorrow'. (There is actually some debate as to whether languages such as English and German really have a future tense, but this debate centres on the question of form rather than function.) (4)

Gattegno Caleb Gattegno, American educationist. Founder of the LT method known as The Silent Way (q.v.). Principal publication relating to LT: *Teaching Foreign Languages The Silent Way*. (8)

General Purpose Course By contrast with 'special purpose' or 'specific-purpose' course (q.v.), a language course which is not linked to any immediate communicative needs for the TL. (8)

Goal/Goals Term often used in sense of aim/aims (q.v.), but sometimes in more specific sense of objective/objectives (q.v.). (14)

Grading The placing of teaching materials, learning points, etc. into a sequence according to their difficulty.

Grammar In narrower sense, means the same as 'syntax', i.e. the structure and form of sentences, and their study. In wider sense, popularised through the work of Chomsky (q.v.) refers to the totality of linguistic rules specific to a given language and the native speaker's knowledge of these rules. (2)

Grammar-Translation Method A LT method emerging in 'purest' form in the nineteenth century in which the TL is taught through the presentation of the rules of the language in a sequence purporting to work from simple to complex, and through practice in applying these rules through the translation into the TL of sentences in the mother tongue. Concentrates on the written word, and teaching is through the medium of the mother tongue. The rules taught are generally prescriptive (see under *prescription*); little attention is paid to the everyday, colloquial usage of native speakers. Most people exposed to this sort of method in the current century have in fact been exposed to a modified version of it including an oral element. Sometimes referred to as 'the traditional method'. (8)

Grammatical syllabus A syllabus (q.v.) which focuses on the grammar of the TL, breaking it down into its constituent parts, and arranging for teaching to be sequenced from 'simple' to 'complex' forms. (14)

Group Dynamics The sum of the ways in which members of a group interact, and the relationships between them; the study of such interaction. (8)

Halliday Michael Halliday, b. 1925, British linguist, Professor of Linguistics at University of Sydney, Australia. Originator and foremost exponent of Systemic Grammar (q.v.) (also referred to as 'systemic linguistics' and 'Hallidayan linguistics'), the major British school of linguistics. His publications include: *Intonation and Grammar in British English*, *A Course in Spoken English: Intonation*, *Explorations in the Functions of Language*, *Learning How to Mean: Explorations in the Development of Language*, *Languages as Social Semiotic: The Social Interpretation of Language and Meaning*.

Hardware In educational technology (q.v.), term referring to any capital equipment such as tape-recorders, TV monitors, slide-projectors. (13)

Humanistic Techniques A term popularised in recent years in the USA to refer to LT techniques (q.v.) which purport to respect and maintain the personality and integrity of the learner, and thereby to enhance motivation. (8)

Hymes Dell Hymes, American sociolinguist and social anthropologist. Though perhaps not the first to use the term, is generally credited with the popularisation of the notion of communicative competence (q.v.). Seminal publication on this topic: 'On communicative competence'—paper first published by University of Pennsylvania Press in 1971, since reprinted, in slightly edited version, in: J. Pride and J. Holmes (eds.), *Sociolinguistics*, Penguin Books, 1972. Extensive extracts also in: C. J. Brumfit and K. Johnson (eds.), *The Communicative Approach to Language Teaching*, Oxford University Press, 1979.

Hypothesis In connection with language acquisition, an initial, but not necessarily, or even usually, conscious, 'formulation' of some aspect of the rules of a language in the mind of the learner, made on the basis of 'observation' of instances of the language to which he is being exposed. Progress towards competence (q.v.) in the language being acquired is thought to entail successive series of hypotheses, or interim 'formulations' of the rules, each stage representing greater approximation towards full competence.

Idealisation In linguistics, idealisation is the portrayal of language or aspects of language as they are in principle, rather than as they are in reality as measured by the speech characteristics of given individuals. Static (q.v.) descriptions of language in particular cannot be other than idealisations; if linguists were to try to take into account all individual variation and all performance (q.v.) factors, it would be difficult to make any significant generalisations at all about the features of a language and the knowledge of it shared by its speakers. (2)

Idiom Language usage peculiar to a certain individual or language community; an expression whose meaning cannot be deduced from the meaning of the individual words of which it consists—e.g. 'Bill is over the moon', in the sense that he is very pleased. (4)

Imitation and Practice As LT techniques, imitation, or repetition, of utterances modelled by the teacher followed by practice, either in the form of further repetition or of drills (see under *drill* and *pattern drill*), have been in use for many centuries, especially with children, who have long been held to possess great imitative capacities and to learn best by 'doing'. Formal, as opposed to pragmatic, justification for imitation and practice appeared to derive from behaviourist psychology (see under *behaviourism*, above) which regarded them as procedures fundamental to the learning of all behaviour. (7)

Immediate Memory The mechanism for retaining limited information over short periods. Synonymous with 'short-term memory'. cf. *long-term memory* and *working memory*. (11)

In-Service Training Training provided for teachers already in employment as such and fitted into evenings, weekends, vacations, etc. (14)

Individualisation The organisation of learning and teaching in such a way as to allow the abilities, interests and needs of the individual learner to be enhanced as effectively as possible, with the consequence that the traditional notions of the 'average student' and 'aiming for the middle' in teaching are abandoned. (8)

Indo-European The family of languages which includes English, and is composed of the Germanic, Celtic, Italic, Baltic, Slavic, Greek, Armenian, Hittite, Tocharian, Iranian and Indic groups. Formerly also referred to as the 'Indo-Germanic' languages. (2)

Infinitive Form of the verb (q.v.) which does not indicate tense (q.v.) or person (q.v.). In English, generally expressed as 'to' followed by the verb—e.g. 'to do', 'to make', 'to be'. (7)

Innate Refers to inborn, as opposed to learnt, behaviours and characteristics. Whether and to what extent language is innate is a current issue in psycholinguistics (q.v.). (7)

Innovative Used in linguistics in the same sense as 'creative'. See under *creativity*, above. (7)

Instrument Term sometimes used in the sense of 'test'. (12)

Instrumental Motivation In context of LL/LT, motivation (q.v.) to learn a language not so much because one is interested in the language itself, but because knowledge of it will lead to the fulfilment of some other important personal objective—e.g. a more interesting job, a posting abroad, a higher salary, etc. Contrasts with 'integrative motivation' (q.v.). (11)

Integrative Motivation In LL/LT, motivation (q.v.) to learn a language because one finds this inherently interesting and/or because one wishes to a greater or lesser extent to 'integrate' into the target society rather than simply because learning the TL will bring material benefits or the realisation of personal goals not directed connected with the language. Contrasts with 'instrumental motivation' (q.v.). (11)

Integrative (Global) Test Any test which purports to test knowledge and use of language in a global way, on the assumption that language represents an integration of skills which work together rather than the sum of items which have been learnt in isolation. Contrasts with 'discrete-point test' (q.v.). (12)

Interference The process whereby the phonological/phonetic, syntactic, lexical and semantic features of the native language impose themselves upon the TL—e.g. if, in speaking French, an English person uses the word 'car' where 'auto' or 'voiture' would be appropriate, this would almost certainly result from lexical interference from English; or, if a Spanish speaker says 'he go' instead of 'he goes', this is likely to be an instance of phonological interference from Spanish. (2, 7, 11)

Interlanguage A concept first proposed by Larry Selinker to characterise the language spoken by a learner as a 'dialect' made up of elements of both the native language and the TL. (11)

Interlocutor One's partner or 'opposite number' in a dialogue or conversation.

Interrogative The grammatical term for a question-form, such as 'Is Bill coming home this evening?'. Contrasts with 'declarative' (q.v.). (8)

Intonation The sound pattern of utterances, produced by variations in the pitch (q.v.) of the voice. (3)

Intuitions In the context of linguistics, term used to refer to the tacit knowledge of, and 'feeling' for, a language possessed by its native speakers such that they can spontaneously judge whether a sentence is grammatical or ungrammatical, acceptable or unacceptable.

Labio-Dental Term used to describe a sound formed with both the lips and the teeth—e.g. English [f] and [v]. (3)

LAD Hypothesis Hypothesis put forward in the work of Chomsky (q.v.) that the human being possesses a special mental faculty or mental organisation, referred to as the Language Acquisition Device, permitting the acquisition of (the first or native) language as an automatic, pre-programmed process requiring only exposure to the language in question to trigger it off. This type of mental organisation is claimed to be specific to human beings and innate (q.v.). (7)

Language (i) There is no totally satisfactory definition of a language as opposed to a dialect (q.v.). A language may be regarded from one viewpoint as a particular and distinctive system of speech sounds used for communication and expression; from another as the system of communication through speech (and writing) peculiar to a particular nation, country or community; from another as the sum of all grammatically, phonologically and lexically similar dialects. However, there is no objective measure, since it is in the final analysis the attitude of native speakers which determines where a language begins and ends. On the one hand, German, for example, embraces mutually unintelligible dialects which for political, social and historical reasons it is convenient to think of as part of the same language; on the other hand, while Danish, Swedish and Norwegian are mutually intelligible, they are considered by their native speakers to constitute different languages. (5) (ii) Language as a system and as a faculty of mind, as opposed to 'speech'. (7)

Language Acquisition   A term which, subsequent to the influential work of Chomsky (q.v.) is often used to contrast with 'language learning' (q.v.) to mean the 'natural', untutored 'picking up' of language, especially in relation to the mother tongue. (7)

Language Laboratory A system allowing, minimally, the simultaneous broadcasting of speech directly, through headphones, to each of a group of language learners so that they may each repeat what they hear without disturbing other members of the group, thus maximising opportunity for practice, while at the same time allowing the teacher to monitor each learner individually. The simplest, audio, laboratory, has no facilities for recording material; in the audio-active laboratory students can record the lesson material on individual tape-recorders in order to work on it at their own pace; in the audio-active-comparative laboratory students can record both the lesson material and their own voices in order, in principle, to be able to compare their own performance with that modelled for them in the lesson material. The two latter types of laboratory also allow a greater diversity of exercises than the type without recording facilities. (13)

Language Learning   A term which nowadays tends, by contrast with 'language acquisition' (q.v.), to be used in the sense of learning which is structured and organised in the context of formal instruction.

Language Learning Capacity/Capability   Terms sometimes used for the sum of the factors which constitute the potential of a person to learn a FL. (11)

Lapse   See under *random error*.

Lateral   In phonetics, a sound formed through the blocking of the middle or one side of the mouth with the tongue, so that air passes around or to the side of the tongue—e.g. [1]. (3)

Lax In phonetics, describes a sound which is held to be articulated with comparatively little muscular tension, and which is of relatively short duration—e.g. the vowel [ı] in *fit*. Whether the question of muscular tension is actually involved is a matter of debate. Contrasts with 'tense' (q.v.). (3)

Learning Nowadays often contrasts with 'acquisition'—see under *language learning* and *language acquisition*, above.

Learning Packet A unit of FL materials (which might be written or might be supplied on audio or video tape, or might be a mixture of audio, video and written materials) compiled for the language learner to work on individually or in group-work. The concept is most often met with in the context of individualisation (q.v.) (13)

Lexis Collective term for vocabulary, or the words of a language. 'Lexical items'—words.

Linguistic Categories Classes of linguistic elements such as noun, verb, adjective, subject, object. (4)

Linguistics The systematic and objective study of language by contrast with language studies, which are concerned more with aesthetic or prescriptive (q.v.) questions. (1)

Linking Words/Phrases Words or phrases used to link the sub-parts of a text together—e.g.: 'therefore', 'however', 'be this as it may, . . .'. (4)

Literacy Strictly, the ability to read and write, and in this sense often intended to contrast with 'oracy' (q.v.) but more generally, ability to use language proficiently. (9)

Long-term Memory The mechanism whereby items of information can be retained and recalled over long periods of time. Contrasts with short-term memory (q.v.). cf. also 'working memory'. (11)

Lozanov Georgi Lozanov, Bulgarian psychologist and inventor of the LT method known as Suggestopedia (q.v.). Major work in this field: *Suggestology and Outlines of Suggestopedy*. (8)

Manner of Articulation In phonetics, the way in which a sound is produced (as opposed to the place in the mouth where it is produced)—e.g. to describe a sound as 'voiced' (q.v.) or as 'nasal' (q.v.) is to give a description of its manner of articulation.

Materials The textbooks, tape recordings, films, television programmes, etc. used to teach a language and containing, minimally, instances of the language (though materials often also incorporate explanations, descriptions and exercises). (8)

Meaning   There is no simple or succinct definition of this term. The concept embraces many different ones, which include: *reference*—the relationship between words or phrases and the objects in the world to which they refer; *sense*—the way in which the elements of language relate to each other when combined in sentences or utterances so that they convey a 'message' which they do not convey in isolation; *denotative meaning*—explicit, 'basic' or 'face-value' meaning; *connotative meaning*—implied meaning, evoking particular associations—e.g. both 'residence' and 'cottage' denote 'dwelling-place', but their connotations are quite different. (4)

Memory   The mechanism or capacity for storing and recalling information. See also under *immediate memory*, *long-term memory*, above, and *working memory*, below. (11)

Mentalism   The view that human behaviour is based on rules and knowledge; an approach to knowledge which sees it as a faculty of the mind rather than as a system acquired in a mechanical way. In LL/LT context, contrasts with 'behaviourism' (q.v.) and 'empiricism' (q.v.). (7)

Method   A set of teaching procedures or techniques (q.v.) assembled in accordance with the principles of a certain approach (q.v.) to LT, and used in conjunction with a certain type of syllabus and materials; the sum of the teaching techniques used in a given LL/LT situation. (8)

Mimicry–Memorisation   LT method using imitation and practice (q.v.) as basic techniques, and short dialogues and drills (q.v.) as basic materials. The techniques of Audiolingualism were largely derived from it, but at the same time rendered much more 'strict', e.g. by proscribing the mother tongue explanations of grammatical points which mimicry–memorisation had allowed.

Minimal Pairs   In phonetics, pairs of sounds or sound sequences which differ from each other minimally. The 'minimal pairs technique' is used to establish the phonemes (q.v.) of a language—e.g. by contrasting [pit] and [bit] (in English), we can establish that /p/ and /b/ are separate phonemes by virtue of the fact that [pit] and [bit] do not mean the same thing. In some languages, the difference between [p] and [b], which is that the latter has voice (q.v.), is not contrastive, and there are therefore no separate phonemes /p/ and /b/. (3)

Minority Language   A language used by a minority in the community—e.g. in Finland, in which both Finnish and Swedish are spoken, Swedish is the minority language. (10). In LT, the term is also sometimes used to refer to a FL learnt by a minority of pupils or students in a particular institution or education system by contrast with FLs learnt by the majority.

Mistake See under *random error*.

Mixed Ability Refers to learning and teaching situations in which groups of learners representing a range of different abilities are taught together. (8)

Model (i) In linguistics, refers to an attempt at a representation of what language (or significant features of it) is like in reality—e.g. the 'transformational model' is the representation of language made in Transformational Generative Grammar. (1). (**ii**) In LT, a term for the person who demonstrates the pronunciation and speech patterns of a FL.

Monitor Model The monitor model, or monitor theory, is an aspect of a number of hypotheses put forward by Stephen Krashen in relation to FL learning. According to monitor theory, FLs may be both acquired and learnt (see under *language acquisition* and *language learning*), and knowledge gained through conscious learning of the rules of a language may be used by speakers to 'monitor', i.e. to keep a check on, their spontaneous production of the language and, if conditions allow, to correct or modify this spontaneous production. (7)

Monocultural Refers to a society in which everyone shares the same culture (q.v.) and cultural values. Monocultural countries are not necessarily monolingual (q.v.), however. cf. 'multicultural', below.

Monophthong In phonetics refers to a vowel which is perceived as 'pure' by speakers of a particular language, by contrast with diphthongs (q.v.)—e.g. in English, the vowel sound in *mad* as opposed to the vowel sound in *made*. (3)

Morpheme Language item which conveys meaning and which cannot be analysed into further sub-units which still convey meaning. Sometimes one morpheme will constitute a whole word (q.v.)—e.g. 'do', which cannot be sub-divided into smaller meaning-units, and sometimes a word will be composed of two or more morphemes—e.g. 'unhappy', which can be analysed into 'un' (=not) and 'happy'. (2)

Morphology The constituents and behaviour of morphemes (q.v.), and their study; the form and structure of words in a language, especially in relation to the way this form and structure affects grammatical relationships and meaning—e.g. 'who' as opposed to 'whom' and 'whose', or 'boy' as opposed to 'boy's', 'boys' or 'boys' '. (2)

Mother Tongue/Mother Language Usually, though not always, the first language to which people are exposed by parents and relations and which they learn to speak first, but in any case the language, acquired in childhood, with which an individual most 'identifies' and of which he feels he has the best and most natural command.

Motivation The driving force felt or demonstrated by someone in relation to the carrying out of a given task. In LL/LT term often used in a generalising way to refer to a learner's enthusiasm for and interest in learning the TL. (7, 11)

Multi-Media Laboratory A language laboratory (q.v.) which is not only equipped with machinery for recording and broadcasting sound, but also with the means for projecting visual images via slides, film or television, etc. (13)

Multicultural Refers to a society in which two or more cultures exist side-by-side, and usually also two or more languages. (9)

Multilingual Refers to a society (or institution) in which several languages are spoken as a matter of course; may sometimes be applied to a person who speaks several languages (but cf. *bilingual*). (10)

Nasal In phonetics, refers to a sound which is produced with the nasal cavity open, i.e. not closed off by the raising of the velum (q.v.), so that air may resonate in it—e.g. [m]. (3)

Needs Analysis An investigation, in the light of a specification of the tasks a learner or group of learners will be required to perform in the TL, of what particular aspects of the TL need to be learnt in order to bring about proficiency in these particular tasks. The results of the needs analysis can then be used to determine a syllabus and suitable teaching techniques. (8)

Neurolinguistics A relatively new branch of linguistics which sets out to investigate the relationship between language and the structure and functioning of the brain and nervous system. (7)

Norm (i) The mode of speech and the grammatical usages held to be most representative of a language, i.e. the 'standard language' (q.v.); the form of a language as spoken by (educated) adult native speakers. (8) **(ii)** In testing, the norm refers to the average performance on a test, the implication being that candidates tested are ranked with respect to each other on the basis that their performances coincide with, or are better or worse than, the norm.

Norm Referenced Test A test which is designed or used to rank candidates in terms of their performance on it in relation to other candidates rather than designed or used to establish how well they meet the requirements imposed on them by the test to carry out a task or tasks necessitating the use of language. Contrasts with 'criterion-referenced test' (q.v.).

Normative Referring to the norm. The 'normative question' in LL/LT is the question of which dialect, pronunciation, etc. of the TL to adopt as the norm and to teach to learners, and which features of the TL to 'forbid', even though they occur in the speech of native speakers, on the basis that foreign learners are likely to meet with a better reception in the target society if they speak a 'correct', 'polite' and widely acceptable version of the language than if their speech is over-colourful or likely to be judged 'vulgar' or coarse.

Notion A semantico-grammatical category, i.e. a category of meaning such as *time, duration, quantity, location*.

Notional Syllabus A syllabus which is based on an analysis of what *notions* (q.v.) or *meanings* particular learners wish or need to express in the TL, and what language items are required to express these meanings. A full discussion of this type of syllabus may be found in: D. A. Wilkins, *Notional Syllabuses*, Oxford University Press, 1976. (14)

Noun A word or group of words which refers to a person, place, thing or idea—e.g. *man, hospital, book, stupidity*. The name of a person (e.g. *Bill*) or place (e.g. *London*) is a *proper noun*. (4, 7)

Noun Phrase Part of a sentence consisting of a noun and any adjectives (q.v.) applied to it—e.g. *the black jacket, twenty young schoolgirls*.

Novel Sentence In linguistics, a sentence 'created' by a speaker on the basis of knowledge of the rules of a language and which is not a 'predictable' sentence or turn of phrase or one which has been learnt or imitated. See also under *creativity*. (7)

Object The noun phrase (q.v.) which is the 'recipient' or 'target' of the action expressed by the verb—e.g. 'we saw a *swan* on the lake', 'I've just heard *a very funny story*', 'do you like *him*?'

Objective/Objectives Term often used in the same sense as 'aim '/

'aims' (q.v.) and 'goal'/'goals' (q.v.) but for some, 'objectives' contrast with 'aims' in that while the latter represent in a general way what one wishes to achieve in a particular language course, the former are statements of the sub-aims to be met if the aims are to be achieved—e.g. if the general aim of a course is to teach spoken French, the objectives to be met will include such things as mastery of the phonological/phonetic system, learning specified aspects of the syntax of the language, learning relevant vocabulary items, etc.

Official Language The language adopted by a country or state as the medium for all its official business. (11)

Operant Conditioning A type of conditioning (q.v.) in which the experimenter attempts to make some particular response (q.v.) or action *initiated* by an experimental subject (and not by the experimenter) habitual and 'predictable' by reinforcing it. (See also under *conditioning* and *reinforcement*). (7)

Oracy The ability to speak a language fluently and effectively, as opposed to being able to write it. (cf. *literacy*). (9)

Oral Vowel A vowel (q.v.) produced by the resonation of air in the mouth (rather than in the mouth *and* the nasal cavity). (3)

Ordering The placing in serial order of teaching materials, learning points, etc. in accordance with some criterion such as 'easy to difficult' for the purpose of planning the sequence to be adopted in teaching.

Organs of Speech Synonymous with 'articulatory organs'—see under *articulatory*. (3)

Overgeneralisation In error analysis (q.v.), an error resulting from too wide an application of a regularity observed in the TL—e.g. 'I was born*ed* in 1960'.

Pace The speed at which material is learnt or practised in a lesson; the speed at which a lesson proceeds. (8, 13)

Palato-Alveolar Describes a sound produced by placement of the blade of the tongue close to the junction between the alveolar (q.v.) ridge and the hard palate—e.g. [š], as in *she*. (3)

Passive In English (and similarly in many other languages) the form of the verb (q.v.) consisting of the appropriate part of *be* and the past participle (q.v.), and usually allowing the use of *by* + [someone]—e.g. 'Fred *was caught by* the policeman'. Contrasts with 'active' (q.v.). (2)

Past The tense (q.v.) used to express past events—e.g. 'Mary *telephoned* us last night.' See also under *tense*. (4)

Past Participle   The form of the verb (q.v.) used (in English) with the appropriate part of *have* (or in some cases *be*) when referring to events in the past—e.g. 'George has *given* me this book', 'Kate has *broken* her promise', 'Patrick will have *finished* his work in an hour'.

Pattern Drill   A type of LT drill (q.v.), popularised by Audiolingualism (q.v.), in which learners are required to manipulate a grammatical pattern, with the idea that they will in this way learn to 'apply' the pattern across the range of possible instances. The drill starts off with a basic sentence for learners to repeat—e.g. '*Is that* the *man* you saw in the park?'—and then gives cues prompting the learners to make any necessary alterations to the basic pattern and to repeat the pattern in its correct form—e.g. (cue): *men* —(correct response): '*Are those* the *men* you saw in the park?'. (8)

Performance   In general sense, what somebody actually says or does as opposed to what they might be, or might have been, capable of saying or doing, e.g. in an examination or classwork. In the more technical sense, contrasting with 'competence' (q.v.), the actual utterances someone produces and/or the actual use of language as opposed to knowledge of the regularities of a language. (7)

Person   Referring in grammar to the categories into which pronouns (q.v.) and forms of verbs (q.v.) are divided, depending on who or what is being talked about—e.g. '*I go* to the cinema occasionally', '*he goes* to the cinema occasionally'. English has five persons: I (1st person singular), you (2nd person singular and plural), he, she, it (3rd person singular), we (1st person plural), they (3rd person plural).

Phone   An actual speech sound representing a phoneme (q.v.). (3)

Phoneme   One of the 'ideal' speech sounds distinctive for meaning in a language—e.g. /p/, /b/, /t/, /k/—as opposed to the sounds, or phones (q.v.), which may actually be produced by a speaker on a certain occasion. (3)

Phonetics   The study of the speech sounds of a language, either in relation to their physical properties or in relation to the way in which they are produced by the human organs of speech. See also under *acoustic* and *articulatory*. (1, 3)

Phonology   The study of the way in which sounds are organised in languages into systems which convey meaning (rather than of the sounds which are actually produced in individual instances). (1, 3)

Pidgin A language composed of elements of two or more languages and used only for purposes of contact, and especially for trading, between people speaking different languages, but not serving as the mother tongue or day-to-day language of any group using it. cf. *creole*. (5)

Pitch The auditory property of a note such that it is recognised as 'high' or 'low'. Variations in the pitch of the voice result from variations in the rate of vibration of the vocal cords—the higher the rate, the higher the pitch. (3)

Place of Articulation Refers to the place within the mouth at which a consonant (q.v.) is produced (by contrast with the manner in which it is produced)—e.g. to describe a sound as 'alveolar' (q.v.) or 'velar' is to give a description of its place of articulation. (3)

Plural In grammar, the form of nouns (q.v.) and verbs (q.v.) indicating reference to more than one person or object—*children* is the plural form of *child*; the plural verb-form *go* is used with 'they'—'they go'—and not the form *goes*—*'they goes'. Contrasts with 'singular' (q.v.).

Population In context of testing and research, the whole of the group with which one is concerned or about which one wishes to make statements. How one defines a population will depend on one's purposes at a particular time—e.g. for some purposes it may be all 15-year-old learners of French, for other purposes it may be all 15-year-old learners of French who have been learning the language for at least three years. cf. *sample*. (12)

Practice See under *imitation and practice*.

Prescription As opposed to 'description' (q.v.), the stating of rules about how people 'should' speak and write in the interests of maintaining certain aesthetic or social standards or, in LT, in the interests of ensuring that learners acquire and use only those forms of the TL widely acceptable to native speakers of the language and unlikely to cause offence. 'Prescriptive rules' therefore make statements about standards to be aimed at rather than reflecting what native speakers may actually say. (2)

Primacy of Speech The idea that because children learn to speak before learning to read and write and that because there are speech communities which function without a written form of language speech must be considered more 'fundamental' than writing as a linguistic medium. Primacy of speech assumed the status of a doctrine in the theoretical assumptions underlying both the Direct Method (q.v.) and Audiolingualism (q.v.)

Proficiency In testing, refers to the potential ability of someone to carry out given tasks or assignments. A 'proficiency test' therefore attempts to measure potential ability in relation to a clearly-defined task, e.g. proficiency for using English in connection with flying aircraft, proficiency for following a University course in a given language. (12)

Pronoun One of the class of words in a particular language which can replace a noun phrase (q.v.) already mentioned or about to be mentioned in the same stretch of text. The English pronouns include: I, you, he, she, it, we, they. (4)

Proverb A saying which is part of the 'cultural heritage' of speakers of a particular language which embodies some 'truth' or fact of experience—e.g. 'A stitch in time saves nine', 'Too many cooks spoil the broth'. Is a sub-class of idiom (q.v.), but is 'fixed' in the language, whereas idioms generally are subject to fashion and change over time. (4)

Psycholinguistics The branch of study concerned with the investigation of the mental processes underlying the learning and use of language. (7)

Psychological Reality A linguistic description may be said to possess psychological reality, or to be psychologically real, if it is thought that it reflects the way in which the mind of the native speaker of the language is organised or functions with regard to language. To what extent any linguistic descriptions so far produced may be claimed to have psychological reality is, however, a matter of debate. (7)

Psychology The study of the behaviour of human beings and animals in terms of the internal forces and the conditions of the mind, emotions and body which make them behave as they do. Specialised branches of particular interest to language teachers are Educational Psychology, which concentrates on problems of teaching and learning, and Psycholinguistics (q.v.). (11)

Puberty The period of transition from childhood to adulthood, i.e. between about 12 and 15 years, generally agreed to be a critical transition where LL is concerned, firstly because it often seems to mark the cut-off point for being able to pronounce FLs without an obvious foreign accent, secondly because it seems to mark the perfection of a social identity, which in some individuals militates against the adaptability required to learn FLs proficiently. (7, 11)

Random Error An error (q.v.) which results from an unpredictable, momentary lapse, lack of attention or distraction, etc. and which is not to be traced to a defect in the speaker's competence (q.v.). Also referred to as a 'mistake' or 'lapse'. (11)

Rationalism In linguistics, a synonym for 'mentalism' (q.v.).

Reading Laboratory A collection of reading passages printed on separate cards and arranged in order of difficulty, accompanied by some means of feedback (q.v.) such as comprehension questions, and a chart on which to enter details of learners' progress through the cards. (13)

Realisation Similar in meaning to 'exponent' (q.v.)—the linguistic realisation of an idea is the actual words and structures used to express it.

Recall The recovery, or power to recover, to the conscious mind information stored in memory. (11)

Reciprocal Terms Terms applying to people or things between whom or which there is a two-way or 'opposites' relationship—e.g. husband/wife, sister/brother, superior/inferior. (4)

Redundancy More linguistic information than is strictly necessary in order to convey meaning—e.g. '*he goes*', where the ending on 'go' could be said to be 'unnecessary', since 'he go' might seem to convey equally well who is being referred to. However, it is widely agreed that human languages need some measure of redundancy if they are to be efficient, since language is often used under conditions in which information is 'lost' in transmission; therefore, the more clues there are to meaning, the more likely it is that the meaning will be understood. Those features of a language which 'double up' on information are sometimes called 'redundant features'. (2)

Redundant Error An error (q.v.), or type of error, acquired by a learner on the basis of mis-information given by a teacher or conveyed in teaching materials, and not arising from a learner's mis-interpretation of correct information.

Reference See under *meaning*.

Referent A person or thing referred to. In: 'Jane came home late last night. She was very tired', 'Jane' is the referent of 'she'.

Reflex In psychology, synonymous with 'response'—an involuntary and immediate reaction to a stimulus (q.v.). (7)

Register The form of language associated with or appropriate to a given situation or context; the subject of the study of the relationship between forms of language and contexts. 'Please enter and take a seat' and 'Come in and sit down' both essentially mean the same thing, but the register of the former is more formal than that of the latter. (5)

Register Analysis The process, or product, of attempting to analyse registers (q.v.) and what constitutes them.

Reinforcement A process associated with conditioning (q.v.) whereby the experimenter attempts to ensure that a response (q.v.) or action will become habitual and 'predictable' by its occurrence being 'rewarded' through the receipt of food or some other satisfaction; the actual 'reward' given. (7)

Reliability In testing, the ability of a test to obtain results in a systematic, and not random, way so that, if repeated on the same candidates, it should still place them in the same rank order. (12)

Remedial Teaching Teaching which aims at making up for deficiencies which in theory should have been corrected at an earlier stage.

Response See under *reflex*.

Retention The ability to keep, or the action of keeping, information in store in memory. (11)

Rote Learning/Rote Memorisation Learning by making a deliberate effort to commit to memory lists of words or other items of information not necessarily (or usually) connected with each other through placement in context. (11)

Rule In linguistics, a regular or systematic feature, or pattern, of language. See also under *description* and *prescription*. (2)

Sample Part of a population (q.v.) which is of a sufficiently manageable size to allow research to be conducted on it with a view to making statements about the population as a whole; part of a population used for the purposes of trying out a test prior to using it on the whole population. (12)

Scoring Marking (of tests) and assigning a rank-order or other form of result to the candidates. (12)

Second Language A language which is not the mother tongue of its speakers, but which is a language of the country in which they live and which they use regularly in day-to-day business within their country. Can be a confusing term, because some (especially in USA) use it in the sense of 'foreign language' (q.v.). (10)

Selection In LT, the choosing of texts and other materials for presentation to learners on the basis of their relevance, interest, etc.

Self-Access Term applied to any LL/LT arrangement which allows learners to gain access to materials and facilities on their own initiative and at times determined by themselves. (13)

Semantic Feature One of the concepts associated with or evoked by a word or phrase conveying some aspect of its meaning—e.g. the semantic features of 'boy' may be said to include: +human, +male, −adult. (4)

Semantics Meaning, and its study. (4)

Semi-Vowel Vowel-like sounds which function more like consonants. The major semi-vowels of English are [w] as in '*w*in' and [j] as in '*y*et'. (3)

Sense See under *meaning*.

Sentence Though we may loosely define a sentence as a sequence of words, usually containing a subject and a verb, arranged as a grammatical and semantic whole to form a statement, question or command, there is in fact no definition of 'sentence' (except in terms of the formalism of certain grammars—e.g. S → NP + VP) which is totally satisfactory, even though most people know intuitively what a sentence is. The sentence is, however, a crucial concept in syntax (q.v.), being the basic unit of language for description and analysis. (2)

Sequence An arrangement of words in linear order; sometimes used in the sense of 'sentence' (q.v.). (2)

Short-Term Memory See under *immediate memory*. (11)

Sibilant A high-pitched 'hissing' fricative (q.v.) such as [š] in '*sh*ot' and [z] in '*z*oo'. (3)

Silent Way A LT method (though based on principles not intended to apply only to LT) invented by Caleb Gattegno (q.v.). The major axiom of the method is that the teacher, while exercising control over the process of learning, remains as silent as possible, allowing and encouraging learners to utilise and maximise their own inner resources in coping with the learning task. Uses charts illustrating pronunciation and grammar, and in some versions, coloured rods. Does not rest on any particular LL or linguistic theory, but is based on more general ideas about education. (8)

Singular In grammar, the form of nouns (q.v.) and verbs (q.v.) indicating reference to one person or object—of 'ox' and 'oxen', *ox* is the singular form; the singular verb-form *is* is used with 'he', 'she', 'it'—'it is'. Contrasts with 'plural' (q.v.).

Situational Syllabus A syllabus based on a collection or sequence of 'situations', usually illustrated and conveyed through dialogues, assumed to be typical of those in which learners will need to use the TL. (14)

Skill In LT, any linguistic accomplishment, but usually one which is assumed to be, or be capable of becoming, 'automatic' so that its exercise is spontaneous. See also under *four skills*. (11)

Sociolinguistics The study of language in its social context and of its use in interaction between speakers. (5)

Software Contrasts with 'hardware' (q.v.) and refers to 'disposable' and 'renewable' items such as materials. (13)

Special/Specific Purpose Course By contrast with a 'general purpose' course (q.v.), one that is based on an analysis of the communicative needs of learners and which sets out to meet these needs directly and efficiently. (8)

Speech The manifestation of language (q.v., sense ii) through speech; what people actually say, as opposed to the system underlying what they say. (7)

Speech Act A sequence of speech viewed as a purposive act, i.e. as engaged in to convey a 'message' or achieve a personal goal. (8)

Speech Processing Memory The mechanism for retaining words and speech sequences as actually spoken long enough to allow decoding (q.v.) to be carried out. (11)

Standard Language The dialect or version of a language considered to represent its most widely acceptable and most widely understood form with regard to pronunciation, vocabulary and grammar. (9)

Static A static description of a language is one which assumes that the language does not change from moment to moment and is consistent as between different speakers of it. See also under *dynamic* and *idealisation*. (5)

Stimulus Anything which arouses or excites a response (q.v.) or is used for this purpose. (7)

Stop A consonant (q.v.) whose production involves a complete closure at some point in the throat or mouth so that air pressure is built up, followed by release—e.g. [p] and [b]. (3)

Stress The emphasis placed in speech on certain elements in it. English has both *word stress*, meaning that certain syllables (q.v.) are more stressed than others within the same word, and *syntactic stress*, meaning that major emphasis is placed on those elements in an utterance to which the speaker wishes to give special prominence. (3)

Structuralism (i) An approach to linguistics which concentrates on the outward form and structure of language as opposed to its 'inner structure' or conceptual aspects, and especially, in the context of LL/LT, American structural linguistics of the earlier part of this century, which largely accepted the doctrine of empiricism (q.v.). (7). **(ii)** An approach to literature (and the social sciences) concentrating on form and structure rather than on the ideas and concepts conveyed in it. (6)

Stylistics The study of literature from a linguistic viewpoint; the application to the study of literature of ideas drawn from linguistics. (6)

Subject The noun phrase (q.v.) in a sentence which is 'responsible' for the action or event, or is in the state or condition, expressed by the verb—e.g. '*Geoff* gave me a book', '*the professor* flew into a temper', '*the milk* seems slightly sour', '*she* looked annoyed'.

Suggestopedia A LT method (though based on principles not intended to apply only to LT) invented by Georgi Lozanov (q.v.). The main principle of the method is to enable learners to achieve a state of psychic relaxation in which they can utilise the full extent of their inner resources and thereby learn much more, and much more quickly, than they, or anyone else, might commonly regard as possible. Large stretches of text are memorised verbatim, and it has been claimed that learners can acquire up to 1000 TL vocabulary items in one day. (8)

Surface Structure Term from Transformational Generative Grammar (q.v.), contrasting with 'deep structure' (q.v.) and referring to the structure of sentences as actually produced and heard (or read). (2, 7)

Syllable A language sound, or combination of language sounds, consisting minimally of a vowel (q.v.) or sonant ([1], [r], [m], [n], [g]) and which may or may not be preceded and/or followed by a consonant (q.v.) or semi-vowel (q.v.)—e.g. 'pop' has one syllable, 'poppy' has two syllables and 'popular' has three syllables. *Open syllable*—a syllable not ending in a consonant—e.g. 'pa'. *Closed syllable*—a syllable ending in a consonant—e.g. 'pat'.

Syllabus A plan or 'blueprint' for the teaching of a particular subject specifying minimally the points or matter to be covered and the teaching sequence to be adopted, but usually also specifying materials (q.v.) to be used and techniques (q.v.) or methods (q.v.) to be utilised. (8, 14)

Syllabus Design The process or activity of planning, organising and specifying syllabuses (q.v.). (14)

Synchronic The synchronic study of a language is one which is concerned with it only in its current form. Contrasts with 'diachronic' (q.v.). (1)

Syntax The study of words and sentences and how they combine to express meaning; grammar (q.v.) in its narrower sense. (2)

Synthetic Describes approaches to LT in which the language is broken down into its composite parts, in terms of rules of grammar, etc., which are then taught on a step-by-step basis and in an assumed order of difficulty, so that learning is a process of accumulation of all the parts and one of working towards the 'whole'. Contrasts with 'analytic' (q.v.).

Systematic Error An error which may be traced to, or judged to stem from, the present stage of a learner's (and by contrast with that of the adult native speaker, incomplete) competence (q.v.) in the TL and which is therefore part of the learner's 'system' and not a random error (q.v.). Such an error might be, say, 'goed' for 'went'. (8. 9)

Systemic Grammar An approach to the analysis and description of grammar most closely associated with M. A. K. Halliday (q.v.) in which the grammar is presented as a series of choices in a network which has to be entered at a particular point, after which further choices are available. It attempts to handle language as a dynamic event, influenced by sociological, psychological and textual factors. Introductory reading is provided in: M. Berry, *An Introduction to Systemic Linguistics: 1 Structures and Systems*, Batsford, London, 1975, and M. Berry, *An Introduction to Systemic Linguistics: 2 Levels and Links*, Batsford, London, 1977.

Target Language The FL to be, or being, taught and learnt. (8)

Taxonomic A term (often used by Chomskyan linguists in a deprecatory sense) for approaches to linguistics which concentrate on listing and classifying the surface-structure (q.v.) elements of language, and applied especially to American structural linguistics (see under *structuralism*).

Technical Aids Any electronic or mechanical aids to teaching such as tape recorders, slide projectors, ciné-loop projectors, and so on. (13)

Technique A particular teaching procedure such as the use of dialogues for the presentation of language in a particular situation or of drills (q.v.) for practice and consolidation; a step in, or part of, a method (q.v.), as distinct from a method as a complete set of techniques. (8)

Tense (i) In phonetics, describes a sound which is held to be articulated with comparatively great muscular tension, and which is of relatively long duration—e.g. the vowel [i:] in 'h*ee*d'. Contrasts with 'lax' (q.v.). (3). (ii) In relation to the verb (q.v.), the device through which the temporal relationship between an event and the reporting of this event is expressed—e.g. past tense: 'Jill *visited* us yesterday'; present tense: 'Jill *is* here *visiting* us today'; future tense (but see also under *future*): 'Jill *will visit* us tomorrow'.

Test A measure (of knowledge and/or ability) designed to yield information for a specific purpose and intended to be applied to a specific group of people so that the performance of each individual may be fairly compared with that of the others. See also under *communicative testing, discrete point test, integrative (global) test.* (12)

Text (i) In linguistics, a stretch of connected discourse (q.v.) as opposed to sentences considered individually. (ii) In LT, a piece of spoken or written discourse for learning and study; a 'shorthand' term for a textbook.

TG (or TGG) Abbreviation for Transformational Generative Grammar (q.v.).

Transfer In psychology, the process of transferring, or the ability to transfer, the skills learnt or exercised in connection with a certain task to the carrying out of another, but not unrelated, task—e.g. one might expect some transfer from the prior learning of German to the task of learning Dutch. (11)

Transformation A formal device in Transformational Generative Grammar (q.v.) for showing the relationship between one structure and another one 'derived' from it—e.g. the 'passive transformation' applying to the active (q.v.) to derive the passive (q.v.): 'Pete (Noun Phrase 1) saw (Verb—active) the man (NP2), so NP1 + V active + NP2 'transforms into' NP2 + V passive + by + NP1, so 'The man was seen by Pete'. (This does not correspond in detail to the way a transformation is expressed in the Grammar, but illustrates the general principle.) (2)

Transformational Generative Grammar In general, the school of linguistics initiated by Noam Chomsky (q.v.); more specifically, the approach to grammar initiated by Chomsky. TG is a sentence-grammar which attempts to state the rules by which *all* and *only* (i.e. only the grammatical) sentences of a language may be derived, and to show how sound (or surface structure (q.v.)) and meaning (or deep structure (q.v.)) are linked. Work within the framework of this grammar has produced a number of significant ideas, such as competence (q.v.) and performance (q.v.), which have influenced thinking about LT, and Chomsky himself has claimed that linguistics is a branch of cognitive psychology aiming at the study of the human mind through the analysis of language. See also under *Chomsky*. (2)

Unconditional Reflex A reflex (q.v.) which occurs naturally and spontaneously, and which has not been procured through conditioning (q.v.) (7)

Underlying Structure A term sometimes used for 'deep structure' (q.v.); structure not apparent in the surface manifestation of a sequence of language, but assumed to be implicit in it, or present in the 'history' of its derivation from more basic structures. (7)

Use By contrast with 'usage' as the set of conventions governing the way language is spoken and written, the dynamic, spontaneous adaptation of it to express and negotiate meaning. (5)

Utterance A speech sequence; a unit of connected speech by contrast with a sentence (q.v.) as a unit used in the syntactic analysis of language. (2)

Validity In testing, the measure of the extent to which a test fulfils the purpose it claims to fulfil. (12)

Variable Any factor present in or affecting people or situations which varies in quantity or intensity either in itself or as between different people and/or situations. Important variables in LL/LT include the age and the previous LL experience of the learner, the methods and materials and the duration and intensity of instruction.

Variant Any alternative or varying linguistic form or spelling; any form varying from the standard. The phrase 'to make the tea' has, in Britain, variants which include 'to brew the tea', 'to brew up', 'to mash'. (7)

Velar Describes a sound produced by contact between the soft palate and the back of the tongue—e.g. [k] and [g]. (3)

Velum The soft palate, which may be raised to block off the nasal cavity.

Verb One of the class of words or groups of words indicating an action or event or the existence of a state or condition—e.g. 'run', 'happen', 'be', 'seem', 'get up'. (2)

Verbal Behaviour The behaviourist (see under *behaviourism*) term for speech and language as a behavioural system. (7)

Vocal Cords A pair of folds in the tissue of the larynx which can be made to vibrate by forcing air from the lungs through them, thus producing the 'voice' of voiced (q.v.) sounds. (3)

Voiced Describes sounds whose production involves the vibration of the vocal cords, including all the vowels (q.v.), and consonants such as [b], [d], [g]. (3)

Voiceless Describes sounds during whose production the vocal cords do not vibrate—e.g. [p], [t], [k]. (3)

Volume The intensity of sound. (3)

Vowel A voiced (q.v.) speech sound produced without friction caused by closing or blocking of the throat or mouth, so that while air under pressure from the lungs can resonate in the mouth and/or nasal cavity, it has relatively free passage. The vowels of (standard British) English are: i (heed), ɪ (hid), eɪ (hayed), ɛ (head), æ (had), ɑ (hard), ɒ (hod), ɔ (hawed), ʌ (hood), oʌ (hoed), u (who'd), ə (herd), ʌ (Hudd), aɪ (hide), aʌ (how), ɔɪ (hoy), ɪə (here), ɛə (hair), ɑə (hired). (Ladefoged's transcription, quoted from: Peter Ladefoged, *A Course in Phonetics*, Harcourt Brace Jovanovich, New York, 1975.)

Words One of the elements of language, generally regarded by native speakers to be the most basic units combinable into sentences (though words can be analysed further into morphemes (q.v.)). Like 'sentence', however, 'word' defies totally satisfactory definition, since the division of utterances into words (for the purpose of writing languages down) is essentially arbitrary and governed by convention, for the sake of convenience, rather than following any 'natural' principles. (2)

Working Memory Synonymous with 'speech-processing memory' (q.v.). (11)

Index

accent, 45;
    foreign, 115f
achievement in language learning, 109
acoustic phonetics, 7
acquisition, see language acquisition
adult versus child language learners, 116f
affective goals, 112
affricates, 28
agreement, 21
aims, 84
allophones, 31
alveolar sounds, 28
approaches, to language study, 4ff;
    to language teaching, 77ff
aptitude for language learning, 109f, 111
articulatory phonetics, 7, 26ff
aspects of the verb, 17
aspiration, 32
association, 61
associative chains, 66
attitude towards language learning, 112
audio-visual aids, 137f
audiolingualism, 81ff, 131, 139f, 141
auditory discrimination, 110, 125

backwash effect of tests, 124
Barthes, Roland, 55
behaviourism, 60ff;
    see also empiricism
Bernstein, Basil, 55, 100, 101
biculturalism in children, 116
bilabial sounds, 29

central sounds, 29
Chomsky, Noam, 66ff, 83
Chomskyan linguistics, 60, 85
cloze test, 131
cognition, 121
cognitive code-learning theory, 85
cognitive development, 58f
communicative,
    approaches, 84, 106;
    competence, 69, 85;
    language teaching, 131, 136;
    needs, 88, 89, 115
community language learning, 86
competence, linguistic, 68;
    see also communicative, competence
concord, 21
conditioning, 61ff
consonants, 26ff
content words, 21
context, 39ff;
    in which target language is learnt, 117f

contrastive analysis, 82;
    syntax, 23
copula, 66
core linguistics, 7
counselling learning, see community language
    learning
course design, see design of language courses
    and syllabus design
creativity, in language, 67f
creoles, 48ff
criterion-referenced tests, 131
Curran, Charles, 86

decoding, 59, 119
deep structure, 18, 65, 67
dental sounds, 29
description versus prescription, 13
design of language courses, 146ff;
    and professional activity, 152;
    see also syllabus design
developmental psycholinguistics, 58
diachronic approach to language study, 7
dialect, 13, 15, 26, 100
dictation, 131
diphthongs, 27
direct method, 80f, 112, 139
disabling factors in language learning, 110,
    117
discourse, 8
discrete-point tests, 130f
discrimination of tests, 127f
distinctive features,
    in phonology, 32;
    in semantics, 38
diversity of language, 93
drilling, 82
drive, 64
dynamic models of language, 47f

educational technology, see technology for
    language teaching
empiricism, 60ff, 120f
enabling factors in language learning, 110,
    117
encoding, 59
English,
    for Academic Purposes, 88;
    as a Foreign Language, 105;
    for Science and Technology, 88;
    as a Second Language, 105;
    for Specific Purposes, 88
error, 87, 114;
    random, 114f;
    systematic, 87, 114

214

Index